TIME MANAGEMENT
(A Study of HRD Managers)

TIME MANAGEMENT
(A Study of HRD Managers)

U. B. SINGH

PUBLICATIONS
KALPAZ PUBLICATIONS
DELHI-110052

Time Management

ISBN: 81-7835-680-5

Published in 2008 in India by
Kalpaz Publications
C-30, Satyawati Nagar,
Delhi-110052
E-mail: kalpaz@hotmail.com
Phone : 9212729499

Lasser Type Setting by: Rudra Computer Graphics, Delhi
Printed at : Singhal Print Media, Delhi

Contents

Preface

None of us is endowed with more than 24 hours a day. Yet, some are able to accomplish more by effective utilisation of time. In fact, time management is life management. If we can utilise this important resource well, all that we manage i.e. our own self, our business and our relationships – would become and continue to remain more productive and vibrant. Effective time management can help improve the quality of life as well.

Human Resource is the resource which is solely responsible for optimising the use of other resources i.e. fiscal resource, material resource etc. Thus optimum use of organisational resources depends upon human capital available to the organisation. The formation of Human Capital is the jurisdiction of HRD Manager. Thus organisational effectiveness is linked to a great extent with the managerial excellence and leadership style of HRD Manager. An HRD Manager has to present himself as a role model in the organisation. The extent of his effectiveness depends upon his management of time.

In this background the present research study was undertaken. This study on Time Management of HRD Managers in public enterprises is probably a pioneer study in the history of public sector in the country, as this aspect has remained unstudied so far. I undertook this academic pursuit for the fulfillment of degree of Doctor of Literature (D.Litt.) in Public Administration, a long cherished desire of mine.

The book is divided into seven chapters. First chapter deals with the importance of human resource in any organisation, and presents an over view of concept and importance of 'time'. The lay-out of the study and universe has also been placed therein. Second chapter describes managing the personal development, while third chapter highlights the concept of effective time management. Managing the time as manager-leader has been discussed in fourth chapter. Fifth chapter throws light on time aspect in managing the decisions. Sixth chapter links time management with life management and seventh chapter summarizes the observations and findings.

Although this academic exercise was intended for a specific purpose, time being important for every one of us to achieve excellence in life, we all would be able to pick a leaf from it and learn to manage our life by managing the time. If we manage ourselves, time will be managed itself. I am sure this humble contribution may help guide a change in the human life. Some one has rightly said that **time is life, don't squander it.**

LUCKNOW **U.B. SINGH**

Ganga Dussehra, 2007

Acknowledgements

This academic exercise is the fruition of many people's efforts. After obtaining my Ph.D. on Human Resource Development, I requested Professor T.V. Rao (a pioneer academician in the field of Human Resource Development) of Indian Institute of Management, Ahmedabad for suggesting a subject for D.Litt. It was he who advised me to study the Time Management of HRD Managers in Indian Public Sector, a virgin area. I found a great guide in him. I can never thank him (I have been unlucky so far not to meet him and express my sincere gratitude in person) enough.

I could complete my research work successfully only because of the excellent guidance I have had from Professor S.K. Singh. I wish to place on record my sincere gratitude to him.

I am thankful to all the HRD Managers and their organisations for extending co-operation in this task.

I am thankful to my learned colleagues and friends at Asian Institute of Technology (AIT), Bangkok, Mizoram University, Aizawl, Administrative Staff College of India, Hyderabad and Lucknow University, Lucknow for their encouragement and constant help in resolving various problems in the way of completion of the work.

I owe my sincere thanks to the library staff at AIT, Bangkok, American Libraries at New Delhi and Kolkata, National Library, Kolkata, ASCI, Hyderabad and Indian Institute of Public Administration, New Delhi for providing books, journals and other materials.

At home, I was a nuisance to my family members, especially to my daughter Nivedita , for remaining confined in my study and not giving adequate time to them. I am thankful to them for tolerating me all those days.

I am thankful to Sri Saurabh Tewari who gave it a proper shape.

My sincere thanks are due to Kalpaz Publications, Delhi for bringing out the book in a record time.

U. B. SINGH

List of Exhibits

List of Tables

1

Prologue

I
HUMAN RESOURCE IN ORGANISATION

Introduction

An organisation is a system of cooperative human activities the functions of which are the creation, the transformation and the exchange of utilities. It is able to accomplish these functions by creating a cooperative system of which the organisation is both a nucleus and a subsidiary system, which has also as components: physical systems, personnel systems and social systems (Barnard: 1968:240). Gullick and Urwick (1937:13) described the basic managerial operations in the following way:

> "Planning... is working out in broad outline the things that need to be done and the method for doing them to accomplish the purpose set for the enterprise;
>
> Organising ... is the establishment of the formal structure of authority through which work subdivisions are arranged, defined and coordinated for the defined objective;
>
> Staffing... is the whole personnel function of bringing in and training the staff and maintaining favourable conditions of work;

Directing... is the continuous task of making decisions and embodying them in specific and general orders and instructions and serving as the leader of the enterprise;
Coordinating... is the all important duty of inter-relating the various parts of the work;
Reporting... is keeping those to whom the executive is responsible informed as to what is going on, which thus includes keeping himself and his subordinates informed through records, research and inspection;
Budgeting... consists of fiscal planning, accounting, and control."

The classical approaches to management were thus viewed as attempts to exploit, control and manipulate workers. In place of the virtues of authority, structure and control, management theorists were emphasising the innate value of the individual worker. Accordingly, management functions were de-emphasised while theorists searched for ways to make workers feel more comfortable and worthwhile in their organisational settings. (Graham & Hays: 1984:25)

Executive positions (a) imply a complex morality, and (b) require a high capacity of responsibility, (c) under conditions of activity, necessitating, (d) commensurate general and specific technical abilities as a moral factor. Every executive, thus, possesses independently of the position, personal moral codes. When the individual is placed in an executive position these are immediately incumbent upon him, several additional codes that are codes of organisation. Codes of organisation are themselves accruals largely of intangible forces, influences, habitual practice, which must be accepted as a whole. These codes are quite different among organisations, being affected by their status, and by their purposes and by their technologies. (Barnard: 1968:272-3) At root, today's public manager is the administrative generalist of Gullick's day, but one who is confronted by a new set of challenges and opportunities.

Neither men of weak responsibility nor those of limited capability can endure or carry the burden of many simultaneous obligations of different types. If they are 'overloaded', ability, responsibility, or morality or all three will be destroyed. Conversely, a condition of complex morality, great activity and high responsibility cannot continue without commensurate ability. Managerial work, on the other hand, is undergoing such enormous and rapid change that many managers are reinventing their profession. Faced with extraordinary levels of complexity and interdependency, they watch traditional sources of power erode and the old motivational tools lose their magic. Competitive pressures are forcing corporations to adopt new flexible strategies and structures. As a result, the ability of managers to get things done depends more on the number of networks in which they are centrally involved than on their height in a hierarchy. In the emerging organisation, managers add value by deal making, by brokering at interfaces, rather than by presiding over their individual empires. It was traditionally the job of top executives or specialists to scan the business environment for new ideas, opportunities, and resources. This kind of environmental scanning is now an important part of a manager's job at every level and in every function. Every manager must think cross-functionally because every department has to play a strategic role, understanding and contributing to other facets of the business.

As managers and professionals spend much time working across boundaries with peers and partners, their negotiating skills become essential assets. Alliances and partnerships transform impersonal, arm's length contracts into relationships involves joint planning and joint decision making. In the collaborative forums that result, managers are more personally exposed. It is trust that makes partnerships work. The sense of ownership alongwith a definite time frame, can spur higher levels of effort. (Kanter: 1989: 85-92)

Leveraging the Human Resource

In the post-liberalisation of economy, Indian industry will need to change the way it operates in order to become competitive. The process begins with a review of business strategy to test it for its soundness in an environment of intense global competition. The value creating ability of the organisations needs to be enhanced and sustained through appropriate strategic initiatives, backed by efficient use of resources. Governance systems need to be put in place to assure the various stakeholders that the organisation's objectives are being met and that resources are being used for the purposes for which they were intended. (AIMS: 1999:90)

In Indian organisations, to leverage human capital for competitiveness much will depend on their ability to nurture knowledge and entrepreneurship. This indeed is what will give Indian corporations the organisational capability to compete in a globalised environment. Leveraging knowledge is the key if organisations are to derive value from new technologies and processes and to forge value creating linkages between processes, business units and core functions.

The future will belong to those managers who are able to create it, to reinvent it, managers who are capable of changing the rules of the game. who can think discontinuities, outside familiar frameworks and who are comfortable with ambiguity. Managers who are not satisfied with success but continue to strive towards doing things even better, who are willing to continuously learn and experiment. Managers who are comfortable in multi-cultural environments and can think globally. (AIMS: 1999:120) These are the qualities required to remain contemporary and be relevant in the years ahead.

Organisations play a crucial role in the lives of the individuals. The behaviour of individuals is mostly dictated by the organisational structures under which they work. Conversely, individuals affect the organisational processes and thus there is a perceptual action and reaction between the individual and the organisation. In actual practice, the organisational structures dominate the behavioural pattern of individuals. Most of the evils from which the society suffers accrue largely from the defective institutional structures or economic systems under which people function.(Singh: 2001:40)

Business organisations with their own cultures operate within societies having their distinctive cultures. As long as the organisations draw their requirements of human resources from societies and operate within those or other societies, the cultural influences across the organisations and societies are inevitable.

With the changed global economic scenario, more and more managers would be called upon to manage jobs in organisations operating internationally, in diverse cultural environments. To be able to manage their jobs effectively these managers must, of necessity, have competencies to appreciate the cultural variables not only of their own organisations, but also of those in societies within which their organisations operate. For these managers, behavioural sensitivity with cultural self awareness and cross cultural awareness thus becomes a required core competency in managing their jobs across the boundaries of their organisations. To be able to manage cross-cultural situations effectively, therefore, managers must not only be sensitive to human behaviour, but also have strong professional and human values, in addition to having other managerial competencies as may be required. (Shetty: 2001:538-9)

The Manager and his Work

A manager-leader is sensitive to the fact that a principal means to 'return on investment' is 'return on individuals'. The job of the manager is to be constantly concerned with performance, proficiency, productivity and profit. This in turn is the product of two factors: the competence of the work group, multiplied by its motivation. In a sense, half of the manager-leader's task is to seek persistently to raise the competence level of his people. The second factor has to do with the manager's ability to motivate his people to become self starting achievers. Over and beyond this, the manager's role is that of a change agent, introducing innovations that will enhance the performance and promote the improvement of his work group, changes that would not occur in his absence. (Cribbin: 1972:4)

Thus, a manager has two specific tasks- the task of creating a true whole that is larger than the sum of its parts, and a productive entity that turns out more than the sum of the resources put into it. This requires the manager to bring out and make effective whatever strength there is in his resources – and above all in the human resources – and neutralize whatever there is of weakness. It requires the manager to balance and harmonise three major functions of the business enterprise: managing a business, managing managers, and managing workers and works.

Liberalisation of economy has made the market more competitive. Old time companies find themselves amidst other competitors- domestic and global. The knowledge of the market has to be deeper, making information an important requirement in management strategy. That calls for a dynamic manager. Dynamic manager is some one aiming at attaining goals at an increasing rate. Being a mere achiever is not enough, every manager must be one. However, achieving at a constant rate causes stagnation. A dynamic manager cannot afford a plateau, he must better his past each year. (Halan: 1999)

During times of global recession, organisations are considering a paradigm shift of focus in terms of restructuring their overall business to beat the competition. No one can dispute that the business turn around requires major reshuffling and a shake up of bloated organisational structures. Gone are the days where bureaucratic and top management centric organisations could succeed. Today, top management is progressively moving towards a more advisory role to perform as catalytic change agents to be able to affect positive ripples in the organisation. Decision making and adaptation to rapidly changing economic and technological needs call for quick and wise strategic initiatives. (Basu: 1999)

As industrialisation takes place, there is a cultural change in regard to the value attached to time. Economic considerations bring about this change. Overall, there is a close correlation between economic growth, industrial advancement and the importance people and the government of the country, attach to time. The successful manager of the future has to change his understanding of the value of time alongwith creating competitive abilities. Increasing productivity of all resources and cutting costs, are essential conditions for the manager of the 21st century. (Bhargava: 1999)

Managerial work in the era of globalisation is undergoing such enormous and rapid change that many managers are reinventing their profession. Competitive pressures are forcing corporations to adopt new flexible strategies and structures. In a growing number of companies, horizontal ties between peers are replacing vertical ties as channels of activity and communication. Companies are asking corporate staffs and functional departments to play a more strategic role with greater cross departmental collaboration. Such a situation calls for an effective and efficient use of time – personal as well as organisational.

Managing Managers

Management's principal function is to make a productive enterprise out of human and material resources. Concretely, this is the function of managing managers. It is clear that resources capable of enlargement can only be human resources. All other resources stand under the laws of mechanics. Man, alone of all the resources available to man, can grow and develop. (Drucker: 1954:12) To manage mangers is therefore to make resources productive by making an enterprise out of them. And management is so complex and multi faceted a thing, even in a very small business, that managing managers is inevitably not only a vital but a complex job.

There is one major factor in every management problem, in every decision, in every action, but an additional dimension: time. The time dimension is inherent in management because management is concerned with decisions for action. And action is always aimed at results in the future. There are two reasons why the time dimension is of particular importance in management's job, and of particular difficulty. In the first place it is the essence of economic and technological progress that the time span for the fruition and proving out of a decision is steadily lengthening. The second peculiar characteristic of the time dimension is that management has to live always in both present and future. (Drucker: 1954:15)

II
TIME: CONCEPT

Time is a resource different from all other resources. It cannot be accumulated like money or stored like materials. It has to be spent usefully or uselessly, at a fixed rate of 60 minutes per hour or 3600 seconds per hour or 86,400 seconds per day. Once time is lost, it is lost and what is really lost is part of our life.

Time is a mystery. It cannot be tied down by a definition or combined inside a formula. Like gravity, it is a phenomenon that we can experience but cannot understand. Neither philosophers nor scientists have been able to analyse and explain all of the meaning of time. Not only have they failed to provide easy explanations, but their efforts sometimes seem to have made mystery more mysterious and to have shown us that our lack of understanding was even greater than we supposed. (Sharp: 1981:1)

Psychological Aspects of Time

Time is a dimension of our experience and our activity, but this dimension does not correspond to a simple physical reality. The concept of time is imposed on us by our experience of changes: the physicist and the biologist must introduce a parameter to account for the evolution of natural phenomenon. Analysis of our experience and the requirements of science show that two fundamental aspects must be distinguished in the concept of time: (a) the sequence, and more precisely, the order of the changes; (b) the duration of the changes or of the period between them. The interlocking of order and duration defines the process of the change.

The psychology of time begins with Kant. Prior to him, the reality of time had not been questioned, even though philosophers disputed its nature. Kant declared that our notion of time is not imposed by a non- menal reality but by the activity of the mind: it is one of the forms of our sensibility. In nineteenth century, in a departure from Kant's essentially rationalistic approach, men became concerned with the actual study of sense of time and with perception of time, and no longer merely with the time of phenomena. A psychophysics of time was developed by comparing estimates of durations with the measurements given by chronometers. Henry Pierson, (1923), was the first to define the psychology of time in a behaviorist framework, through the objective study of human behaviour in relation to time. This point of view was developed by Pierre Janet (1928), who raised the question of our adaptation to time. Jean Piaget ((1946) studied the development of the notion of time in the infant. Paul Fraisse (1957) provided a general analysis of temporal behaviour. (Fraisse: 1963)

Some philosophers have argued that the passage of time is an important metaphysical act, but one that cannot be grasped by non-rational institution. Others feel that the flow of time is an illusion and that the future can no more be changed than can the past. Some believe that future events come into existence as the present, the actual 'moment-in-being' reaches them; others suggest that they are already in existence. (Shackle: 1958:13-14)

Social Organisation of Time

Since all human activities occur in time, the existence of a social system necessitates some organisation of time. Such organisation entails: (a) systems of time measurement, based upon cosmic and human cycles, (b) the allocation and scheduling of time by individuals, and (c) a set of attitudes toward time past, time present, and time future. But if time is not necessarily an explicit category, it is always an aspect of experience, implicit in thought and speech. The experience of time takes two major forms – sequence and duration. From the stand point of sequence, events are seen as located in particular order along a moving continuum. The experience of duration derives from the relative span of events and of the intervals between them. The experience of time as a continuum is often compared metaphorically to the movement of water, sometimes the linear flow of a river, sometimes the cyclical ebb and flow of the ocean; indeed the English word 'time' has the same root as 'tide'.

But above all, attitudes toward time present focus upon the alternative uses of time that are offered by an elaborate division of labour, the minute scheduling that this division of labour entails, and the continual presence of a watch upon the wrist, which makes man ever conscious of the fleeting moment. In most literary traditions, writers express their regret at the passing of pleasure and the shortness of human life, but it is the perpetual concern with the passage of time that is characteristic of industrial man. Made aware that time is his scarcest resource, he learns to 'spend' and 'save' it like money. The ideology that stands at the centre of industrial society stresses the full and productive use of time, a commodity that requires the most careful husbanding. This concern is as characteristic of socialist systems as of capitalist systems. Managers often find that the behaviour of newly industrialized workers in developing countries deviates sharply from these enunciated values. (Goody: 1963)

Time in Economics

Time is a scarce resource, although in a rather special way. Time, in a sense, is inexhaustible. We do not know when it began and we cannot understand how it may end. No one knows the size of his remaining pile of time and it cannot be hoarded. As Shackel(1958:15) describes: "The moment-in- being" rolls, as were, along the calendar – axis, and thus ever transports us willy nilly to fresh temporal viewpoints. Since the scarce resource of time must be spent, a basic problem of human existence is to spend it well, to use to bring in the greatest return of happiness that can be achieved. (Sharp: 1981:2)

A classical appraisal of the treatment of time in economic analysis may be found in Hicks. The discussion concentrates upon the treatment of time in relation with the 'self contained ness' of the 'single period' (Hicks: 1985). Mandelbrot (1997) has introduced a distinction between 'clock time' and 'trading time'. Landesmann and Scazzieri maintain that the analysis of time in economics suggests a principle of 'relative invariance' grafted upon the distinction between slow and fast moving components of the economic system. (Encyclopedia: 2001:1655-6)

Time has been regarded as a form of input required in production using capital equipment by those who have followed Bohm-Bawerk in regarding the use of machinery as a round about method of production. The only direct mention of time in

Samuelson's standard text book on economics is a reference to time being consumed in indirect method of production, followed by the argument that "Economic activity is future – oriented ....current productive efforts... produce for the future in order to repay the past for present consumption." (Samuelson: 1948:46-7) Another attempt has been to put a money value on the time savings that arise from transport improvements.

The analysis of varied views expressed by economists in regard to time shows that there is no single clearly defined concept that comes into the mind of economists when the word 'time' is mentioned in relation to their subject. Shackle (1958:94) is concerned with the argument that the static state is a useful theoretical concept whereas that stationary sale is useless and unrealistic, since it involves seeking to 'put time in fetters or rob it of its essence'. It is apparent that, for Shackle, time is synonymous with change. He is not concerned with the problem of allocating the scarce resource of time except in so far as uncertainty is involved. Since we cannot make decisions about the past, all economic choices relate to the future and uncertainty exists. But the degree of uncertainty about using time is not necessarily greater than that associated with the consumption of any other goods or service. Time in economics, for Shackle, would be abolished if there was no economic change. But time is a scarce resource and individuals will be forced to make choices about its use in this world so long as man is neither omnipresent nor immortal. (Sharp: 1981:10)

Time: Source of Competitive Advantage

Like competition itself, competitive advantage is a constantly moving target. The best competitors, the most successful ones, know how to keep moving and always stay on the cutting edge. Today, time is on the cutting edge. The way leading companies manage time represent the most powerful new sources of competitive advantage. In facts, as a strategic weapon, time is equivalent of money, productivity, quality, even innovation. Managing time has enabled top Japanese companies not only to reduce their costs but also to offer broad product lines, cover more market segments, and upgrade the technological sophistication of their products. These companies are time-based competitors. After World War II, variety- driven Japanese companies pioneered time-based competitiveness. They managed structural changes that enabled their operations to execute their processes much faster. As a consequence, time became their new source of competitive advantage.

Today's new generation companies compete with flexible manufacturing and rapid-response systems, expanding variety and increasing innovation. A company that builds its strategy on this cycle is a more powerful competitor than one with a traditional strategy based on low wages, scale or focus. These older, cost-based strategies require managers to do whatever is necessary to drive down costs. The tactics used reduce costs but at the expense of responsiveness. In contrast, strategies based on the cycle of flexible manufacturing, rapid response, expanding variety, and increasing innovation are time based. Organisation structures enable fast response rather than low costs and control. Companies concentrate on reducing if not eliminating delays and using their response advantages to attract the most profitable customers. It has become essential in the post-liberalised and globalised open economic era, when Indian public sector enterprises have to stand competition with multinational companies. Time is a major factor in competitive economy.

For the leading competitors, time has become the overarching measurement of performance. By reducing the consumption of time in every aspect of the business, these companies are also bound to reduce costs, improve quality, and stay close to their customers. (Stalk: 1988:41-51) Time is thus gaining a principal position in determining the competitive ethos and survival strength.

Getting the Best of Time

Most people seldom have enough time to do all the things they want to do. They have to work late in the office, carry papers home for disposal and spend all their energy in the drudgery of daily routine. They have, therefore, no time to plan and execute jobs requiring their personal attention. Nor do they have adequate time for self development. One's control over time is directly related to the hierarchical position one holds in an organisation. Time must therefore be utilised with utmost care and on a priority basis. In the competitive environment prevailing in all spheres of life, the one who manages his time effectively will have the cutting edge. (CM: 2001:553)

In the words of Peter F. Drucker (1961:44) "Time is the scarcest resource and unless it is managed nothing else can be managed." The object of time management is to increase and optimize the use of discretionary time. Time management expert Merril E. Douglass (1975) says that "The way you spend your time determines how you live your life and that is who you are. Tomorrow is connected to today just the same as today be connected to yesterday." The failure to manage time is the result of poor planning and is related to how managers feel about themselves. Broadly speaking, the pattern of time spent in a work situation is closely related to the personal values and priority system of an individual. (Saxena: 2000)

While time is a basic business performance variable, management seldom monitors its consumption explicitly. Yet time is a more critical competitive yard-stick than traditional financial measurements. Many an organisations are now realizing the need of a time manager on the lines of fiscal manager, sales manager, materials manager, human resource development manager etc. Indian public sector is now recognizing the importance of time. It is of utmost importance in the post-liberalised economy. The entry of multi-national companies in Indian economy is leading to the era of competitiveness. Time is a main factor in emerging market economy. Public sector has to produce quality goods/services with less investment of money and time. The human resource thus has to be oriented to the changing environment. Hence, there is an emerging emphasis by HRD Managers on effective management of time.

III
LAY OUT OF THE STUDY

Scope of the Study

Organisation is a place where resources – human, fiscal and material come together. Managers are responsible for acquiring, organising and combining resources to accomplish goals. The optimisation of fiscal and material resources depends much upon managing human resource, a flexible one having different personality, characteristics and motives. Thus, a Human Resource Development (HRD) Manager has an edge over his counterparts in the organisation, Fiscal Manager and Material Manager.

In view of the important role destined, accomplishing the goals of organisation depends much upon HRD Manager. Organisation is a living organism, with 'time' an important factor. It becomes, therefore, pertinent to study the pattern of managing the time by a Manager who is also an individual human being in addition to being responsible for managing human resource in an organisation. Beyond working hours he has a lot of time and varied tasks. The timely performance of tasks and the use of 'free time' or 'discretionary time' sometimes create a challenge before every individual. The study covers the patterns of managing the 'committed' as well as 'discretionary' time by HRD Manager.

Universe

Although the technique of human resource development in India owes its origin to the private sector, a good number of public sector organisations have created a separate HRD wing. In many cases the Personnel Manager has been rechristened as HRD Manager and traditional personnel functions are treated synonymous to HRD functions. In few organisations even human resource development is concentrated only to training and development activities. As such, an attempt has been made to widen the coverage of the study to public as well private sectors and produce a comparative study. The thesis however rotates around the HRD Managers working in public sector enterprises. The experiences from private sector are added to make the study more fruitful.

Methodology

It was primarily a case study method of research. The public sector organisations engaged in varied sectors, like production, service, and development formed the universe.

The study is based on primary as well as secondary data. Primary data were collected through a structured questionnaire. The secondary sources consisted of books, journals, reports etc.

In addition to HRD Manager or Personnel Manager or the person responsible for managing human resource, the management boards, managers, peers and subordinates were also contacted on selective basis and their views/observations on various facets were obtained.

Limitations

It was not possible to conduct personal interviews hence questionnaire was mailed to the individual Chairman/Managing Director/HRD Manager for furnishing the data. The inherent shortcoming of mailed questionnaire was observed, hence a few HRD Managers were personally interviewed and their routine observed minutely. Despite best persuasions and concerted efforts, the respondents were found not forthcoming and willing to divulge the pattern of use of their discretionary time. Most of them were found conscious and cautious while responding. The responses related to use of even committed time (time spent in office) were very general and vague. There was almost uncertainty about the use of discretionary time (time beyond office hours).

Although about 150 HRD Managers from various public as well private sector enterprises were intended to cover and as such the structured questionnaire was mailed to them. The response was however not enthusiastic and adequate. Time having been treated as personal property of an individual; the officials divulged the pattern of its use related to the hours fixed for working. Hence subsequently method of participatory research was adopted and some 50 HRD Managers were selected and closely observed, each for a week. The study thus concentrates on the responses received from 50 HRD Managers, and the report has been developed on the basis of pattern of time used by these officials.

The main body of the thesis depicts percentage distribution in place of absolute numbers.

IV
ABOUT THE UNIVERSE

As a part of participative research the personal characteristics of the selected officials were collected-age, qualifications and experience being the focus areas. Although data were collected sector wise (public as well as private), the analysis has been made combinedly in view of the intention of the scheme to study the pattern of managing time by HRD Managers.

Age of Respondents

Age of the respondents forms a basic characteristic. The dynamism, innovation and creativity are supposedly the focal strength of a young manager. The analysis (Table 1.1) reflects that about one-fourth of the manager respondents were over 55 years of age and all have reached to the position by virtue of their length of service in the organisation. Such a trend is prevalent prominently in public sector enterprises. It is encouraging that more than half or to be specific three managers out of five belonged to middle age-group (35 to 55 years). Every seventh official was found quite young i.e. at initial stage of career. It is observed that units falling in private sector are infused with young blood contrarily to their counterparts in public sector, whose first preference is experience due to length of service put in over the merit of the officials.

Table 1.1
Age of Manager Respondents

Age-Group (years)	*Numbers*	*Percent*
25-35	7	14.00
35-45	15	30.00
45-55	15	30.00
55 and over	13	26.00
Total	50	100.00

Educational Qualifications

Academic soundness provides a solid ground for easy grasping and rapid development. A suitably qualified person easily appreciates the problems. The analysis concurs with the general observation of attracting qualified and meritorious persons towards private sector. A number of factors are responsible for such a situation. It is significant that about one-fourth of the managers had obtained high degrees in Business Administration. About one-third had studied Personnel Management and another one-fifth opting for Labour and Welfare subjects. A few engineers were also found managing the human resource in these enterprises. The data reflect that private sector enterprises attract persons having studied Business Administration or MBAs. In public sector units managers have acquired the degree in the area of personnel management probably during their service as a prerequisite for their elevation to the higher positions.

Table 1.2
Academic Background of Managers

Qualifications	*Percentage Distribution*
M.A.(Labour & Welfare)	20.00
M.A.(Personnel Management)	34.00
Engineering	6.00
M.B.A.	26.00
Others	14.00
Total	100.00

Sex

Sex of an individual is another important factor affecting the use of time. Although the highest law of the land treats male and female at equal pedestal, women are far behind their counterparts in many aspects of life. The recent past has witnessed an initiation of empowerment of women, but they still lag behind. Unfortunately, out of 150 HRD Managers having been surveyed and 50 out of them intensively interviewed and their routine closely observed, there was only one female HRD

Manager. She was comparatively young but energetic and inquisitive. She extended all sorts of cooperation in survey work. Although such a meagre number cannot help draw any trend, it is a recognised fact that women have to perform many roles at home and an equally challenging task at office. They are hard pressed of time in view of role conflicts. They are thus more conscious and practical about use of their time.

References

Barnard, Chester I. (1968), The Functions of the Executive, Harvard Business University Press, Cambridge, Massachusetts.

Graham, Cole Blease and Hays, Steven W. (1984), Managing the Public Organisation, Washington D.C.

All India Management Association (AIMS) (1999), Indian Business (Strategies for Competitiveness), Amexcel Publishers Pvt. Ltd., New Delhi.

Shetty, P.N. (2001), The Challenges in Managing Business under global Competitiveness, in P. Rao (ed.), WTO & Competitiveness, Excel Books, New Delhi.

Gullick and Urwick (1937), as quoted in Barnard, C.I.(1968), op.cit.

Saxena, Shailendra (2000), Integrated Time Management, Hindustan Times, New Delhi, May 18.

Sharma, Rajiv (1981), Time Management (unpublished mimeo), Training Material, Institute of Public Administration, Lucknow University.

Robinson, John P. (1977), How Americans Use Time: A Social Psychological Analysis of Everyday Behaviour, Praeger, New York.

Sharp, Clifford (1981), The Economics of Time, John Wiley & Sons, New York.

Bell, Daniel (1973), The Coming of Post Industrial Society: A Venture in Social Forecasting, Basic Books, New York.

Douglass, Merrill E. (1975), Creative Use of Time, The Personnel Administrator, October.

Fraisse, Paul (1957) 1963, The Psychology of Time, Harper, New York, as appeared in International Encyclopedia of Social Sciences, 25.

Shackle, G.L.S. (1958), Time in Economics, Amsterdam, North Holland Goody, Jack and Watt, Ian (1963), The Consequences of Literacy, as contained in International Encyclopedia of Social Sciences, 30-42.

Hicks, John (1985), Methods of Economic Dynamics, Clarendon Press, Oxford.

Mandelbrot, B.B. (1997), Fractals and Scaling in Finance: Discontinuity, Concentration, Risk, Springer, Berlin and New York.

Scazzieri, Roberto, (1994), Economic Theory and Economic History: Perspectives on Hicksian Themes, in Herald H. and O.F. Hamonda (eds.), The Legacy of Hicks: His Contributions to Economic Analysis, Routledge, London.

Jonathan, M. (ed) (2001), Encyclopedia of Social Sciences, Vol. IV, Fitzroy Dearborn Publishers, London-Chicago.

Soule, G. (1955), Time for Living, Viking Press, New York.

Stalk, George (Jr.) (1988), Time – The Next Source of Competitive Advantage, Harvard Business Review, July-August.

Competition Master (2001), Effective Time Management, Khanna Bros., Chandigarh, 553-8.

Drucker, Peter F. (1954), The Practice of Management, Harper & Row Publishers, New York.

Drucker, Peter F. (1961), How to be an Effective Executive, Nations' Business, April, 44-46.

Basu, Ranjit (1999), Techno Revolution, Hindustan Times, New Delhi, March 4.

Halan, Y.C. (1999), The Dynamic Manager, Hindustan Times, New Delhi, March 11.

Kanter, R.M. (1989), The New Managerial Work, Harvard Business Review, November-December, 85-92.

Cribbin, James J. (1972), Effective Managerial Leadership, American Management Association, Inc.

Singh, Sunita (2001), Globalisation and National Development, in P. Rao (ed) WTO & Competitiveness, Excel Books, New Delhi, 29-46.

Bhargava, R.C. (1999), Watch Your Step, Hindustan Times, New Delhi, March 11.

Samuelson (1948), in M.Jonathan (ed) (2001), Encyclopedia of Social Sciences (2001), Fitzroy Dearborn Publishers,London – Chicago.

Linder (1970), as quoted in Robinson, J.P. (1977), How Amercians use time: A Social Psychological Analysis of Everyday behaviour, Praeger, New York.

2

Effective Time Management

In the early days of civilization when man was living in caves and wandering in jungles, he hardly had any necessity to care for his time. But with the continual 'development' of civilization to the extent of today's mad rush, the scarcity of time is being felt severely almost by everyone and that is why the necessity of its management has arisen.

Total Cycle Time

Time is the most potent weapon in the arsenal of competitiveness. Time is the crucial factor in determining cost, productivity and asset utilisation. People are inspired to improve if they believe the performance improvement goal is desirable and realizable, and if they can see a believable methodology to reach that goal in a reasonable time. Total Cycle Time is a system of utilizing efficiently the time that elapses from the moment a customer expresses a need until that need is satisfied. Within that time span are many individual cycles. In most businesses, cycles of activity fall within three interlocking areas: manufacturing and marketing, design and development, and strategic thrust (Thomas: 1991:2), as depicted in Exhibit 1.

Exhibit 1
Cycles of Activity

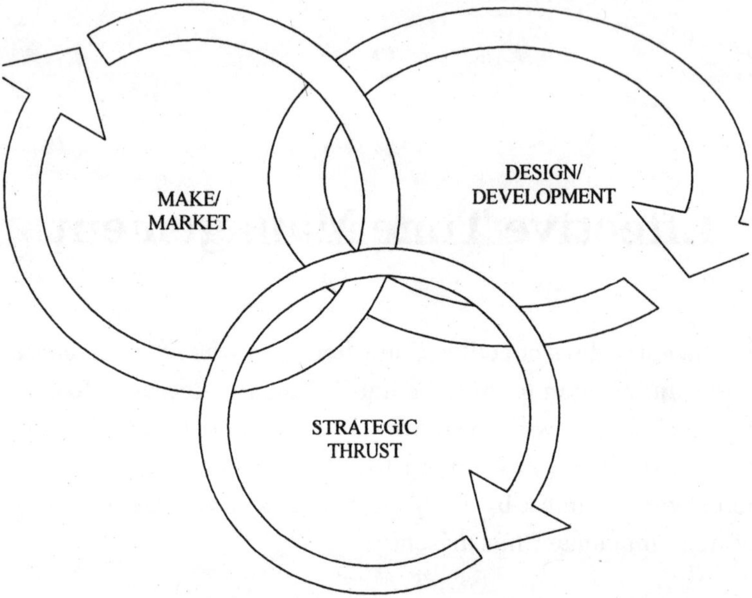

In almost every company there is substantial gap between its accustomed performance i.e. baseline, and its achievable performance i.e. entitlement. Achieving entitlement does not require the addition of new resources. It is a matter of eliminating barriers to responsiveness and time to market. Barriers come in three types: one is subject matter - counter productive activity or processing problems. The second barrier lies in the business process itself - the detailed steps a company follows to complete the business process. Process barriers can be very tough to detect because they are part of a company's accepted procedures. The third type of barriers are cultural - accepted corporate mind set – measurements, controls, incentives, values, or mythology that prevents decision makers from seeing the woods for the trees. (Bajaj: 1998: 34) Total cycle time thus requires no speeding up of effort, no additional resources. Instead, it's a matter of using what you have more effectively.

Shorter the cycle times, more are the opportunities there to learn from experience and make improvements. Systematic exploitation of cycles of learning is one of the most potent, yet neglected, areas of opportunity in any organization. It is therefore essential that every business cycle contains a system of measurements, on going feedback loops to apply the lessons of experience, and management forcing functions. Cycles of learning are a way of life in any entitlement company. They improve upon themselves, pushing performance higher and higher.

Three Rs define competitiveness and the relationship between speed and better performance. They are – Responsiveness, Results acceleration, and Resource effectiveness. Responsiveness is a matter of a company being able to react to customers' needs precisely, economically and quickly with minimum resources. Results acceleration is a matter of a company systematically using its cycles of learning to continuously improve its performance, particularly in the areas of quality and cost, and shorten its cycle times. Resource effectiveness, which results from short cycle time thinking, simplified business processes, and cycles of learning, is a matter of getting the most performance with the least capital, people and inventory. (Thomas: 1991: 2-16) These three are mutually supporting and are the very essence of competitiveness

An organisation that reaches and maintains its entitled performance level undergoes a five stage process. The stages are – Inspiration, Identification, Information, Implementation and Institutionalization. Although they overlap somewhat, they are basically sequential.

Exhibit 2
Total Cycle Time: The Five Is Process

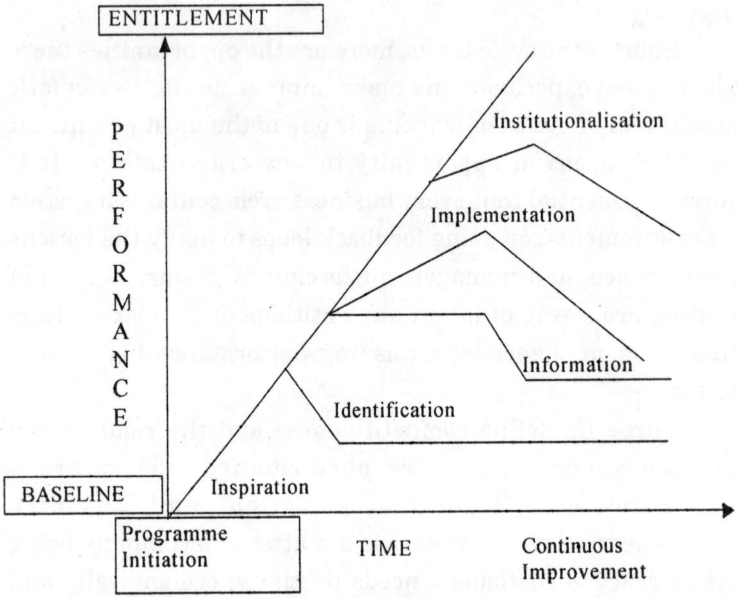

Source: Adapted from Thomas (1989) & Thomas and K.R. Martin (1991)

Turning an organisation around begins when people at the top get the spirit, but the concept motivates others down the line the same way. That's the Inspiration part. Once the spirit is willing, one moves into the Identification phase, in which it zeroes in on the various cycles within its design/development and make/market loops and identifies the baselines and realizable performance levels in each. As that process unfolds, an organisation begins its Information phase, in which the appropriate skills are transferred to the people as necessary to identify barriers, exploit the lessons of experience, and shorten cycle times. Which, of course leads to action: the Implementation phase in which the barriers are removed. The final phase begins while Implementation is underway and never really ceases: Institutionalisation (as shown in Exhibit 2). Thus total cycle time amounts to a cultural change for a company, so, in the final phase of its turnaround, it must forever embrace the ethics and the habits of the new culture, in the same way as it would have to make quality improvement a way of life. Quality improvement, incidentally, is part of the total cycle time package. (Thomas: 1991:186-7)

Time Budgets

Many interesting pattern of social life associated with the temporal distribution of human activities – with regularities in their timing, duration, frequency and sequential order – are explored in literature on time use, time budgets, and time allocation. Such accounts examine how people spend their time within the boundaries of a working day, a week end, a seven day week, or any other relevant period. There is time measured from the movements of planets and time measured by the rate of radio-active decay. And for our purposes there is the much more limited and comprehensible concept that we may call human or economic time. This is the time that human beings have at their disposal and that must be allocated between alternative activities.

People cannot use the same lump of time to carry out more than one or perhaps two activities. But most activities demand an exclusive consumption of time. The time during which we exist must be allocated between all the alternative and generally mutually exclusive activities that are available to us. Robbins (1945:15) argues that "The time at our disposal is limited. There are only twenty four hours in the day. We have to choose between the different uses to which they may be put". This view- point is generally accepted today, but nevertheless some uses of time seem to have regarded as being different from others so that separate models have been developed for dealing with time in which paid work is done and with leisure time. A utility maximizing exercise would involve allocating time in such a way that the marginal utility of the last unit spent in each activity was the same, and it would be necessary to include all type of activity. (Sharp: 1981:4)

Gross (1984:519-58) discusses from an anthropological perspective, the significance of time allocation studies among social scientists. He states several benefits derived from the use of time allocation studies, which provide important data concerning attitudes, values, cultural style, and emotions. Any behaviour with an observable environmental effect can be observed using time allocation techniques, including speaking, working, relaxing and leisure. Robinson(1997) argues that time use provides insight into the values, society and the individuals within its place upon work, raising children, mobility, and the search for a better life. (Harvey and Holler: 2001: 1657-9)

Many of the references to time in economics are not concerned with its allocation but use time as a proxy for change. It is also a convenient unit for 'spacing out' measurements of economic indicators such as those relating to output, prices and wages. The American economist George Soule was one of the first writers to deal extensively with the time allocation issue. Soule (1955:89) argues that economists have not developed a comprehensive theory for dealing with time as a scarce resource and that 'economic theorists' have not absorbed the concept of time into their basic thinking. The best known basic study of time allocation is probably contained in Becker's article 'A Theory of the Allocation of Time' which was published in 1965. (Sharp: 1981:11)

Theory of Time Allocation

The basic assumptions of this analysis are that time is in some senses the ultimate scarce resource and that the most fundamental economic decisions made by an individual are about how we will allocate the future time that he expects will be available for his use. (Szalai: 1966) Most of the difficulties and complications arise because of the existence of various limitations on the freedom of choice. The main restrictions that may affect the free allocation of time may be described as being legal, institutional or organisational, climatic, the effect of prior decisions, the required cooperation of other people, and the need to possess market goods or to be able to command market services. Legal restrictions may forbid some uses of time or enforce others. The institutional and organisational restrictions on the use of time may have an economic basis or be mainly the result of custom. Their effect is to lead the fixed hours, which are not determined by the consumer, during which consumption, or the pursuit of an activity, is possible. The most important organisational restriction on time use is the limitation on shopping imposed by having shops open only at fixed hours. Climatic limitations on time allocation are fairly obvious, and in as far as they cannot be altered is no special concern of the economists. However, if the climate cannot be changed, its effects can sometimes be overcome. (Sharp: 1981: 18-21)

The freedom to allocate time to specific activities is limited as the result of many previous allocation decisions. Another restriction on the freedom of allocating time to some activities arises because the agreement and cooperation of other people may be required. Much of the attention on the economic analysis of people's behaviour in allocating their time, has centred around the need to undertake paid work in order to earn money which can be exchanged for the market goods that are required as direct or indirect inputs for other non-work activities. (Meier: 1959)

Time Allocation Model

The basic problem in the use of time is not choice between work and leisure, nor is it the allocation of leisure time or free time. The fundamental issue is to consider how time can be allocated between all available activities so that maximum utility can be obtained. The simplest situation is where the allocation decisions relate to a specific short time period, where there is no uncertainty and where the market goods input constraint is eliminated. (Nakanishi: 1963)

Economists are accustomed to thinking of individuals as consumers of goods and services who can maximise their satisfaction by an efficient allocation of their money resources. Time is an additional constraint that has been examined by a few specialist writers, but its importance is usually largely ignored in the analysis of the behaviour of consumers. The availability of money, or the power to obtain a supply of market goods and services, then becomes the additional factor that must sometimes but not always, be considered. When money resources are more than adequate for any required input of market goods, consumers only need to allocate their budget of time between alternative activities, all of which have the same time price in a way that will maximise utility. After short listing the activities, he would then maximise his utility by allocating his time between the activities so that the marginal utility of the last unit of time allocated was the same in all activities and no gains could be made by any reallocation of time. (UNESCO: 1966)

It must be assumed that marginal utility diminishes for all activities as the amount of time allocated to them increases, other wise all the available time would be devoted to the activity with the highest initial utility ranking. (Sharp: 1981:26)

The degree of complication is found when money income cannot be increased and is insufficient to buy all the inputs that would be required if time was allocated to all the preferred list of activities, but where the inputs for each activity have a fixed money cost that does not vary with the amount of time that is allocated to them. The next complication that arises is that the money cost of an activity may vary directly with the quantity of time that is allocated to its pursuits.

Factors Affecting Time

In order to put into perspective and to gain a greater understanding of the myriad factors that determine the allocation of time, interest in time use shifts rapidly away from the single distribution of time figures to more detailed analysis of their internal structure. In this conceptual framework, time use is portrayed as being determined by four sets of factors: personal, role, resource and environmental. All four sets of factors are treated as mutually interacting. (Robinson: 1977:27)

Most basic of the factors are the personal factors, such as the person's sex and age. These, in turn, are linked closely to the social role requirements that people assume, the main time relevant ones being imposed by the responsibilities of employment, marriage and parenthood.

Role factors, in turn, interact with two other sets of factors: environmental factors such as societal scheduling or ecological location, and resources, such as income and home technology. Environmental factors may be seen for the most part as constraints on the individual's use of time, and resources may be seen as largely providing more options for the use of time. (Exhibit 3)

While personal, role, resource and environmental factors all directly affect the way time is spent, so does time itself. For example, quite apart from the effects of these four factors, individual decisions about time allocation ultimately determine how much time is available for other activities. As Linder (1970) notes, work time "affects both the supply and the demand for time on other activities".

The most straight forward interpretations of time use data can be made by economists who take at face Benjamin Franklin's maxim 'time is money'. With their central concern about productivity, it seems only natural that economists would recognise the function of time to capture many of the 'productive' transactions of daily life. (Robinson: 1977:3-4) The increased value of time was also a central feature of Linder's (1970) treatise on The Harried Leisure Class, although he started from a

Exhibit 3

Schematic Model of Factors affecting Time Use

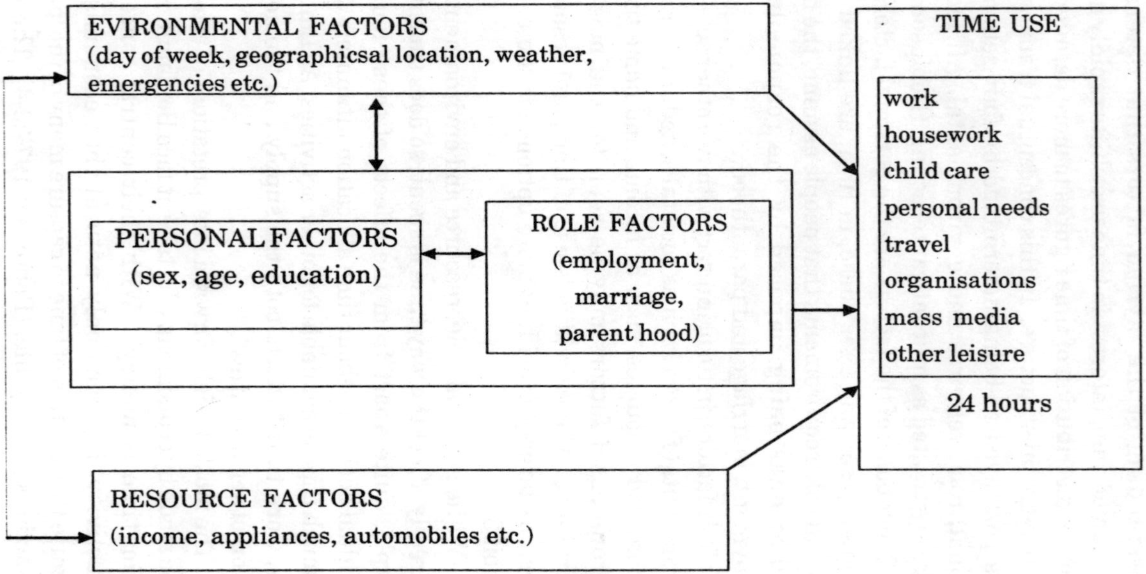

Source: Adapted from Robinson (1977), 28

different set of premises. However, the profundity of our dependence on time goes beyond those aspects of time captured in econometric models. Indeed, concern about time is also considered one of the earmarks of a 'post-industrial society'. (Bell: 1973:4)

Perhaps more promise for the time variable in sociology lies in treating time as a measure of 'territoriality'. Melbin (1976) developed this analogy most extensively, noting parallels in human behaviour and distinguishing three major mechanisms – queuing, phasing and scheduling – by which humans use time to communicate with one another or to compete with another. (Robinson: 1997:5)

Some researchers, like Gutenschwager (1973), have suggested that time be treated solely as an input, with the output in the form of choice of activities. As such, time can be viewed as a basic human resource with the attractive property unlike other national resources; it is equally distributed to all members of society. Inequalities thus only arise from the energy levels people invest and the productivity they derive from these constant amounts of time. This is also reflected in the phenomenon of secondary activities such as use of time to simultaneously accomplish two or more objectives.

The HRD Managers were asked as to whether they maintain any record of spending their time at office or at home or both. Astonishingly, none of the respondents has any data collection or any instrument for recording the time. In absence of any proper mechanism, it was not possible to ascertain the time allocated and actual time spent on each task. A mix of responses and observations having been made (even for a week only), is quite reflective of the time use of HRD Managers in public sector enterprises (Table 2.1).

A few managers admitted to prepare data collection chart, but response could not be substantiated. It seems they have no clarity of the mechanism. A good number of managers felt any such chart was not required. They however could not produce convincing arguments in their support. Engagement diary is a sole mechanism regarding time use and control. More than half of the managers admitted to allocate time to each activity but criteria as disclosed are either past experience or guess work. Total ad- hocism is practiced in this regard.

Since managers lack personal sense of time no record is maintained on actual time spent on each activity. It seems employees are free to take their own time because there is no mechanism applied for controlling the time except the past experience on such activity or guess. Thus every task and activity is necessary for almost all managers who feel all the tasks part of their duty. They don't treat any activity as time wasters. They find their time used properly and not wasted. This reflects the lack of knowledge and concept of HRD managers about use of time, time budgeting, free time, time robbers etc. They all need to be oriented in this regard.

Systematic Planning of Time

Time is a unique resource and must be handled uniquely. Without efficient handling of time, no amount of ability, skill or experience will make one effective in life. Management of time through persistence and determination alone is omnipotent.

The first step in the management of time gives the data of one's time utilisation. ABC analysis can be applied to this data to group the tasks routinely carried out into three parts:

1. Those few tasks that account for a bulk of time utilisation form the A group. About 20 per cent of the tasks that account for 80 per cent of the time used is classed in this group.
2. The B group may contain another 20 per cent of the tasks that account for 10 per cent of the time used.
3. The C group contains the remaining 60 per cent of the tasks that may use up the remaining 10 per cent of the time.

Table 2.1
Data Collection on Time Allocation

Activities	*Responses (Percentage Distribution)*	
Prepare Data Collection Chart	Yes	15
	No	60
	Not Required	25
Mechanism to Control Time	Engagement Diary	95
	Memory	2
	Not Required	3
Do they allocate time to every activity	Yes	60
	No	25
	Not Required	15
Criterion for allocating time	Guess work	25
	Past Experience	75
Whether actual time spent is recorded	Yes	20
	No	80
How time use is controlled	No proper mechanism	80
	Based on experience	70
	Employees take their own time	60
	Not possible	30
	Not required	20
How to identify time wasters	All activities necessary	95
	Part of duty	80
	Little time is wasted	90

It is obviously not very useful to increase the efficiency of time utilisation for C group of tasks. On the other hand improving efficiency of time utilisation for the few tasks in A group is likely to help considerably in time management.

Hibbard and Landrum (1978:256) say: "Even though planning does consume time on the front end, it overcompensates both by bringing in better results and saving time in actual performance of activities. So take time to plan and do not engage in crisis management. In order to properly plan and determine priorities, use either end of each day to set daily goals, ranking them by their importance. To make the planning of daily goals, effective priorities must be established. By scheduling your time effectively through prioritizing, you learn to avoid over committing yourself".

By keeping a time-control chart a manager can find how he is spending his time and what activities are taking most of his time. This chart is a simple piece of paper on which the tasks desired to carry out are listed. Every morning he can prepare the list of tasks he desires to carry out on that day under two heads: Musts and Shoulds. 'Musts' are the essential tasks which have got to be carried out on that day; 'shoulds' are tasks that may be carried out if time is available on that day. Against each task he should note the estimated time requirements and ensure that the total required time does not exceed the time available for performing the tasks. There may be transfer of some items from one head to the other but it is vital to ensure minimum such changes. Too many changes often mean inefficient use of time. It is important to control the intervention of others in planning of time.

When the day is over, the various tasks carried out should be marked along with the actual time spent on each of the tasks. The analysis of the data should be carried out periodically. This will help in effective utilisation of time.

The well organised life leaves time for everything- for planning, doing and follows through. Time is not used up in regretting or in trying to live life retroactively, or in an explaining way something needed has not been done. (Royal Bank: 52) The real point of managing time effectively is to carve out as satisfying and rich a life as yet possibly can. (Bensahel: 1979:60) Porter (1978: 58) observes that "Time is life, life is time; you waste your time, and you waste your life: you control your time, you are in control of your life". Thus self discipline is the key to managing time.

Keeping the importance of planning the day in view, the officials were requested to divulge whether they plan their time. The responses (Table 2.2) are quite revealing. All the managers were found unanimous not in planning the day but they have some record of engagements for the day, particularly fixed for the office hours. Although about one-third managers expressed that they plan their personal time, it was however not substantiated. As regards planning the working hours, they felt the duration fixed and all the engagements duly recorded.

Planning pre-supposes role clarity and specific objectives. The managers in general often lack these. They never bother to prepare the list of tasks to be performed and hence no planning. The managers do memorize the important and urgent works to be done during the day. But everything is moving in an ad-hoc manner. Systematic planning of the day is necessary for effective management.

Planning the day for most of the officials is confined to attend the meetings on time and any other works assigned by the boss. As regards personal or discretionary time, indifference of officials towards importance of time (indirectly to life) finds prominence. It is their sweet will to engage themselves in some house hold chorus. They are found not having any definite agenda for their discretionary time. A few of them spend some time on walking (morning and evening), going through newspapers, watching T.V. etc. Informally, some officials admitted to read newspapers and magazines during office hours as they are either late riser or have difficulty in passing the time during the working hours. It is ironical that the managers are apathetic to major portion of their time. Managers working in private sector enterprises are however found having some concern about their time, at least of committed hours. It may be because of competitiveness in industry and insecurity in career.

Table 2.2

Whether Managers Plan their Day

(Percentage Distribution)

Types of Time	*YES Great Extent*	*Some Extent*	*NO*	*No Response*	*Total*
WorkingHours	70	20	10		100
Personal Time	10	20	50	20	100

Many of the public sector managers often face problem in passing the time at office. They have definite working hours but they devote only a portion of committed time towards accomplishing the organisational goals. They are part of the hierarchical organisation and lack initiative and creativity. If anyone dares, the rules create hurdles, some times initiatives boomerang. They just therefore follow the instructions received from superiors, undertake the tasks assigned and order the subordinates. Their counterparts in private sector have a definite role to perform and goal to accomplish. They seem more concerned about their responsibilities. It seems that once in job, many managers confine their role just to finish the tasks assigned and take rest at home. They often fail to link time with life. The effective time management presupposes effective life management. Once life is organised time will follow the suit. Thus self-discipline is a major determinant of time management.

Problem of Self- Discipline

The analysis of various research studies undertaken world over gives four patterns of time utilisation. The first pattern is when, on most days, a large number of 'musts' are not carried out while many 'shoulds' have been carried out. This is essentially a matter of self -discipline.

When a person is setting priorities, he is very rational, and he puts in priorities for those items which are really important. However, when he starts working, many non-priority tasks consume his time and priority items remain unattended. This may happen for many reasons. Some priority tasks might be unpleasant. The task might be difficult and the person is not clear how to carry out the task. Another reason why one gets distracted by non-priority tasks is because they are interesting.

The basic approach to improve self-discipline is to determine taking up the tough tasks one by one and refuse to divert to other tasks until it is completed. Self-discipline is the most difficult step in time management, while it is the most important one too. It is impossible to improve time management significantly by other steps- since, in the absence of self-discipline, the time saved is quickly frittered away in unnecessary activities.

Management by Crises

The second pattern revealed by analysis of time control chart of people, who concentrate on 'musts' but still have 'musts' left over day-after-day although they have not been diverted by any of the 'should' tasks. These are the 'overloaded people' who are heading into trouble. They find urgent tasks becoming 'immediate' and 'very immediate' and ultimately becoming crises and they get into the habit of 'managing by crises'. These crisis managers can be a menace in an organization.

The 'overloaded people' ought to take another look at their 'must' tasks and ask three questions – (i) How many of these tasks really ought to be done? It will be found that many of the tasks which have been given priority by tradition are not really necessary. (ii) How many of these tasks are to be done by me? How many can be delegated? It would be found that many of the tasks can be delegated to reduce pressure on time. (iii) Am I spending too much time on each of these tasks? This leads to the review of efficiency in using time.

The crisis managers are detrimental to an organization. Their time management problem eventually becomes an organizational effectiveness problem. They make the organizational culture a crisis culture.

The Empty Plate

The analysis can reveal a third pattern of people who finish all their 'musts' and 'shoulds' by lunch time and have nothing on their plate after lunch. This represents bad allocation of work by the boss or lack of imagination and initiative on the part of the executive himself in understanding the potential scope of his job. An intensive discussion by the executive with his boss is indicated and this can lead to a new division of work that can make the executive's job more meaningful.

There are very few people who are able to tackle most of the 'must' jobs day-after-day and also attend to a few 'should' jobs now and then. Such people have no time discipline problem and are in control of their time.

In this backdrop, the respondent managers were asked as to whether they list out the tasks proposed to be undertaken during the day, prioritise them and classify them as must, should, ought, urgent, important. The purpose of such a question was to determine how priorities were established and by whom. In absence of any planning the managers never classify their tasks. They give priority to urgent rather than important matters.

Every work is rated by them as important. The manager's only aim is to follow the rules and regulations. It was hence necessary to substantiate this general feeling. The responses are self speaking (Table 2.3).

It is surprising that a little number of managers prepare any list however, a good number prioritise their tasks. But every priority is disrupted when any other directives are received from the top management. In public sector top managers generally set the priorities of their immediate subordinates. The letters are marked as 'Most Urgent', 'Urgent', 'Immediate', 'To-day' etc., and the subordinates are obliged to act accordingly. Their own priority of tasks is superseded. Since enterprises largely run (leaving aside actual production place where machines operate) through papers and the urgency of paper works is marked by higher management, the work priority is determined accordingly.

Most of the managers are at either end of the spectrum, i.e. either they establish the priorities or the top management does it. Many a time, managers get orders from the top management and their lot of time is spent on completing the tasks thus assigned. In public sector culture everything comes from top to down and the priorities are set accordingly. A very little scope is available at middle and operational levels to stick to the priorities, if any made. In such a bureaucratic model of public sector organisations every one is obliged to carry out 'on top priority basis' the wishes of the superior irrespective of the need of the hour in connection with work or the organisation. The rules, regulations and wishes of top management run the writs in public sector enterprises. There are however certain exceptions, depending upon approach of the individual top executive. The managers on the other hand don't bother to take any initiative and creative step. The situation needs proper redressal and a turnaround.

Although managers expressed that they prepare a list of tasks, prioritise them and work accordingly, in reality, no list is

Table 2.3
Tasks Planned and Prioritised

(Percentage Distribution)

Items	*Yes*		*No*	*Not Required*	*No Scope*	*Total*
	GE	*SE*				
List of tasks is prepared	10	20	60	10	-	100
Tasks are prioritised	40	20	30	10	-	100
Who sets priorities						
Boss	10	20	70			100
You yourself	40	30	30			100
Self discipline practiced	15	25	10	15	35	100
Management by crises	10	30	25	15	20	100
Work load adequate	20	30	50			100
Work load less	5	15	30			
Overloaded	20	10	20			
Work done according to priority	20	40	30		10	100
Superior's orders prevail upon your priority	60	20	20			100
Initiatives are taken by you	20	20	10		50	100
Work is planned	20	25	20	15	20	100

GE - Great Extent SE – Some Extent

prepared. Every subordinate acquaints the manager with the pending work or the work he proposes to take up for the day. The manager either concurs or suggests certain alterations. Basically, he is supposed to do every thing but nothing particular. This is some what reflective as many organisations treat HRD functions synonymous to traditional personnel functions of hiring the employees, train them, protect their interests and gives incentives etc. If the technique of HRD was understood in correct perspective and applied in proper way, the managers really will be having a lot of responsibilities and roles to perform.

Data collection sheet is an important mechanism for allocating time for each task according to priorities. Management by crisis should be minimized and instead welcomed as priority. Data sheet should have some scope to provide cushion in case of situation of crises arising. Such a chart is necessary to control the time daily. In beginning there may be some problem because of factor of self-discipline but after a few days or weeks the self-discipline will prevail upon and the managers can start enjoying the new situation. They can thus, spare a lot of time out of the committed hours and can spend that additional time in any other good work.

Managers can see that the data on time utilisation obtained through the daily time control chart provides important information that can help in improving time management. It can tell them whether their real problem is the self-discipline problem or whether the problem is their drifting into management by crisis, or whether they have the time management problem of the other type i.e. having time but nothing to manage.

Another aspect revealed in the analysis of the actual time expenditure is the 'compulsory idle time'. This is the difference between the total daily working time and the total of the time actually spent on each of the tasks carried out. The idle time is essentially the time wasted in waiting for papers or people. This calls for improving the planning at work.

Time Wasters

Most people blame others for their poor utilisation of time. However, a deeper insight can show that most things that waste time can be traced to our own habits and not to external imposition. An important task in improving efficiency of time utilisation is the identification of time killers. Time killers are activities that kill time continuously.

It is easy to assume that others are solely responsible for the waste of one's time, but if one collects data, he may find that the biggest time waster is he himself, others do waste one's time but very often he aids and abets them and many times wastes his time and their time in collaboration with them.

Mackenzie (1975:75), after a survey in fourteen countries, has identified and chosen the following factors which help in wasting the time:

1. Telephone interruptions
2. Drop-in-visitors
3. Meetings (scheduled and unscheduled)
4. Crises
5. Lack of objectives, priorities and deadlines
6. Cluttered desk and personal disorganization
7. Ineffective delegation and involvement in routine and detail
8. Attempting too much at once and estimating time unrealistically
9. Lack of, or unclear, communication or instruction
10. Inadequate, inaccurate or delayed information
11. Indecision and procrastination
12. Confused responsibility and authority
13. Leaving talks unfinished
14. Lack of self discipline.

Narayan (1999) after making a survey of project managers, has identified following most common time robbers in a project environment:

1. Incomplete work
2. Jobs done over

3. Delayed decisions
4. Poor communications
5. Telephone calls
6. Casual visits waiting for people
7. Failure to delegate
8. Poor retrieval system
9. Impromptu tasks
10. Too many levels of review
11. Union grievances
12. Casual office conversations

All these time-wasters can be grouped under seven principal management functions in which the activity occurs:

1. Planning
2. Organising
3. Staffing
4. Directing
5. Controlling
6. Communicating
7. Decision making.

The time efficiency also depends on one's working habits. Learning when and how to say 'no' becomes important because manager's over-commitment dilutes his effectiveness. Effective managers from time to time close their doors to provide a period of uninterrupted concentration. (Mackenzie and Kau: 1975)

One of the most agonizing problems in time management is the problem of interruptions and consequent fragmentation of time. The working time is so much fragmented that it is virtually impossible to handle anything serious. To tackle the problem of fragmented time the executive must get the support of the organisation. Thus, during the quiet time an executive is 'not available' and this makes him free to attend to serious matters.

The next most important step in organising time is the appropriate handling of papers. There are only three kinds of papers: things requiring action, things to be read and passed on or filed, and things which can be thrown out. Managers should separate his paper work into these categories and then analyse each. Efficient executives dispose of papers without much loss of time. Inefficient executives are reluctant to deal with any matter immediately. Another time-waster is an executive who multiplies paper. Any paper coming to him is multiplied as he sends his response to several persons with copies of the original paper, even when they have nothing to do with the matter. Another time-waster is the one who wishes long responses instead of making simple comment.

In fact, communication becomes management's tool for unifying an organisation's activities whereby corporate goals are achieved. (Rotenbury: 1978:28) Effective communication will achieve clarity, understanding, commitment and creativity. (Hall: 30) Delayed or ambiguous communication acts as a major time-robber. Managers waste lot of time waiting for the communication or getting clear communication.

Procrastination is a major stumbling block for almost everyone seeking to improve his use of time. There are three causes which lead to procrastination: (i) unpleasantness, (ii) difficult projects, and (iii) indecision. Harry Rotenbury (1979: 24) recommends that "Set a deadline for every goal. There is no better way to speed performance". Procrastination through indecision is one of the biggest time -wasters as the same aspect is studied over and over again and is still not disposed of. It can also lead to the problem getting worse and ultimately requiring much greater time to tackle. On the other hand, taking snap decisions can also be wasteful as these will have to be continually revised. Lack of loyalty to one's own decisions cannot only waste time, but also affect adversely the credibility of the person.

It is important to deal with visitors as quickly as possible without adversely affecting the matter to be dealt with or the relationship to be maintained.

Instead of looking at every paper as it comes in or calling a person as manager needs him, the work should be bunched together. This ensures that the interactions are not too frequent and interruptions are minimized once the discipline of dealing with the matters is established. Another way to minimize the number of formal interactions is to have informal meetings at a specific time over a cup of coffee.

An individual executive may be an efficient manager of his own time but he makes others wait for a short meeting with him everyday, he is wasting precious man- hours regularly. In a meeting, or during discussions with others, if a senior executive is prone to frequently digressing from the main topic, he is again wasting an increasingly precious organisational resource, that is, available man-hours for which organisation is paying money. (Saxena: 2000)

Similarly, a habit of sermonizing subordinates repeatedly is not good from the point of view of integrated time management. A bad time manager not only wastes his own time but that of others also. A good time manager on the other hand, if he acts in isolation may be able to manage the time of the total work force well. All managers should know and respect the importance of other's time just as they respect their own time. This means greater need for time management for all or integrated time management. It is true that even in a de-layered environment the time of a senior executive is more important than the time of his junior counterparts. But the time of no one is absolutely unimportant. Therefore, there is a need to ensure that no body's time is wasted in infructuous and unproductive activities.

With this back ground, the HRD Managers were asked to reveal their opinion about the time-robbers. In this regard, the managers feel that majority of their working hours are eaten away by meetings. The managers emphasised that they cannot ignore paper work. The piles of letters received and responded everyday form an important part of every manager's daily committed routine. The visitors (internal as well as outsiders) and phone calls interrupt their functioning. But the managers do not find these interrupters as time-wasters. These, according to them, are part of their duty. They were reminded that these activities really are essential in performing the duties, but many times disrupt the functioning and waste their invaluable time, if not handled properly. The major time- wasters as identified by the managers and proportion of their average time used on these activities are collected in Table 2.4.

Table 2.4
Major Time-Wasters

Items	*Time Consumed (Percentage Distribution)*
Meetings, including preparation	40.00
Letters (Paper work)	20.00
Phone calls	10.00
Visitors	15.00
Others (not specified)	15.00
Total	**100.00**

The average number of hours spent per week on each time-robber indicates the magnitude of the time management problem in public sector enterprises. If 30 to 40 per cent of a manager's time is spent on time- wasters, then this limits him to a maximum of 70 per cent productivity in each time period. However, a few managers feel that time-robbers are simply part of an HRD Manager's responsibility. They treat meetings, phone calls, visitors as a part of their duty, and not time-wasters. These activities virtually help in performing duties successfully but become disruptive only when not managed and handled properly. The managers should plan these activities according to their priorities. These should be fit along the major activities and in no case be allowed to disrupt the smooth functioning.

At this stage managers were further probed and asked to provide a list of works generally done by them in routine in a day. Many a managers out rightly refused to be specific but a good number of respondents made sincere efforts. A list of general routine works done by them every day may look like as under:

1. Going through letters and select important and urgent ones
2. Discussion with immediate subordinate supervisor or deputy to take stock of the situation
3. Follow up of previous day's unfinished works
4. Briefing to the top management or immediate superior
5. Planning to meet the pressing problems, if any
6. Meetings with peers
7. Meetings with subordinate supervisors (team meetings)
8. Planning for the next day
9. Paper work
10. Vending visits/communication
11. Supervising functional works
12. Attending visitors
13. Responding phone calls
14. Other miscellaneous jobs

The majority of the managers feel that they are productive at least six hours per day and productivity lower than this is probably the result of increased time-robbers, or an inability to handle time-wasters. It is an established fact that an individual can have lot of energy, but the productive use of this energy may be low. The average man is usually productive for about six hours in an eight hour work day. To corroborate they were further asked to indicate the time spent on these activities. Although managers were found not maintaining any record of their time use, they made a sincere effort to approximate the time used in varied tasks. The responses are collected in Table 2.5.

Table 2.5
Time Spent Daily on Routine Jobs

Activities	*Time Spent (Percentage Distribution)*
Correspondence	5.00
Taking pre-view of day	5.00
Follow up of unfinished works	10.00
Reporting to top management	5.00
Preparing contingency plans	7.00
Team meetings	10.00
Organisational meetings	15.00
Planning for next day	5.00
Vending visits	5.00
Supervision	5.00
Visitors	5.00
Phone calls	3.00
Desk work	10.00
Serious matters	5.00
Others (including break)	5.00
Total	**100.00**

It is clearly illustrated that managers generally spent about one-third of their committed time away from their desk. While at desk, a good part of their time is eaten away by unproductive works like correspondence, visitors, phone calls etc. They enjoy a little amount of quiet time to take up serious matters and also for planning and thinking.

Principles of Time Management

It is paradox of management that those who are responsible for organising the activities of others often have the most trouble in managing themselves. Time management is nothing more than applying the principles of management to ourselves.

Time is obviously most important resource of executives. Time is altogether unique because its supply is totally inelastic. For organisations, money is usually fairly plentiful, manpower can be hired, raw materials and plant space can be increased, but time is the one thing that no manager can rent, hire, buy or store. (Drucker: 1964-70: 130)

Generally time management is perceived to be a sole preserve of top/senior executives as in common perception executives at other levels are not hard pressed for time. Moreover, time management is supposed to be a job by different individuals for themselves separately and in their individual capacities. When time management is not talked about in the context of individual, it is often mentioned in organisational context with particular reference to project management where 'time overruns' are talked about. But, seldom is an integrated approach to time management considered for implementation. (Saxena: 2000)

Time management is efficiency oriented. It does not provide answers, it only provides time that managers need to solve complex organisational problems. (Mathur: 1993: 96) Professor Less Danielson suggests that managers spend most of their time on activities which interest them, followed by those which they do well, which are pleasurable, and which are least interesting.

The only principle which seemingly is followed by a majority of executives is the Principle of Muddling through – little planning, less organisation and practically no control. The value of managing an executive's time cannot be underestimated. (Moore: 1968:77) Adcock (1970) has developed ten principles of time management from an extensive review of literature on time management. These principles are:

1. Principle of Time Analysis
2. Principle of Daily Planning
3. Principle of Budgeting by Priority
4. Principle of Flexibility
5. Principle of Delegation
6. Principle of Activity Segmentation
7. Principle of Control of Interruptions
8. Principle of Minimization of Routine Work
9. Principle of Plan Implementation and Follow-up
10. Principle of Repeated Analysis

Adair and Allen (2003) suggest another set of ten principles, which aim at self improvement through time management. These principles are:

1. Develop a personal sense of time
2. Identify long-term goals
3. Make medium-term plans
4. Plan the day
5. Make the best use of your best time
6. Organise office work
7. Manage meetings
8. Delegate effectively
9. Make use of your committed time
10. Manage your health

The blocks to effective time management are both external and internal. Alan Lakein (1973) offers some basic ideas about establishing goals and setting priorities. He recommends ranking both life and job goals as: (a) a goal of high value and importance,(b) a goal of lesser importance, such as improving relations with a boss or subordinates and (c) goals of low value. Lakein then offers six suggestions for more effective management of time:

1. List goals and set priorities
2. Make a daily 'to do' list
3. Always start with goals of high value and importance and not the goals of low value
4. Continually ask yourself 'what is the best utilisation of my time right now?'
5. Handle each piece of paper only once
6. Do it now

It is known that mismanagement of time in any activity lying on a critical path may delay an entire project. Therefore it is imperative that proper utilisation of time of the entire work force is ensured. If we do not work towards an integrated time management, the time management methods practiced by individuals may at times work at cross purposes and some individuals for reducing the time required by them in doing specified jobs may end up wasting other's time leading to sub-optimal time management on an overall basis. Now-a-days more than ever before, in the face of increasing competition in the market place we need integrated time management. (Saxena: 2000)

Getting Most Out of Time

Time is cyclical, in which events start, change and stop. The inability to start an event is called reluctance. The inability to change events within time is inflexibility. The unwillingness to stop an event in time is being compulsive. High level executives need to spend never increasing amount of their day on planning and thinking. Planning and thinking includes preplanning for next day's activities, for accomplishing short range goals, and for developing strategies to achieve long- term objectives. It includes setting goals for subordinates as well as providing for their business and personal development within the overall objectives of the company. (Mathur: 1993:99-102)

The experts on subject have suggested many measures to enable the executives getting most out of their time. Some of these are:

Take Time for Planning

Every moment spent in planning saves many hours in executing a task. A manager won't accomplish the things he wants without careful planning. It is the simple, most important step in effective time management.

Set Priorities

At the start of each day, list the jobs one has to do in order of their importance. When one job is complete, review priorities to ensure they are still accurate. At the end of the day, compare what was actually accomplished with what had been hoped to accomplish. Then prepare a list of things to do the next day.

Set Deadlines

Set realistic deadlines and stick to them. To develop an accurate sense of how long it takes one to complete routine tasks, time yourself on regular tasks for one week. Then calculate average completion times.

Tackle one Thing at a time

Forget about everything else until the one task that's on desk is finished. Constantly jumping from one problem to another will eventually destroy the power to concentrate on anything for more than a few minutes at a time.

Use Prime Time Effectively

Determine peak time of the day and devote that time to top priority work. One can accomplish more in less time when he feels fresh and mentally alert, so use that time effectively to work on those things requiring your greatest attention.

Do not disturb

If job is flexible, set aside a part of day when interruptions are not allowed. Don't spend that time on trivial things. Use it for major projects.

Learn How to Make Decisions

The kind of decision required depends on the circumstances. Sometimes a snap decision is needed, while under other conditions, a democratic approach is more appropriate. In either case, identify the problem and gather only as much information as is really needed. Consider the alternatives and their consequences, and then make decisions. If perfection let paralyse, one will never be able to get anything done.

Handle Only Once

As soon as you read any letters reply immediately, while the subject is still fresh in your mind. This saves having to reorient you with the situation.

Use the Telephone

Use the telephone for local call, instead of letter. Communication via telephone can be much more effective than a memo because it creates two – way communication. The main reasons for sending letters are to clarify, remind or confirm.

Reply on the Original Letter

For routine in-house correspondence, jot your reply on the top or side of the memo you were sent. This way the receiver has both the question and answer on one piece of paper.

Make all Your Calls at Once

If you have a number of telephone calls to make, place them constructively. In the long run, it will be quicker than disrupting your work flow through the day.

Get out of Circulation

It is vital to keep in touch with what's happening in the organisation and the industry, but being on too many circulation lists uses too much valuable time.

Set Time Limits on Meetings

If you are planning a meeting, provide an agenda and clearly define the purpose and objective of the meeting. Set a time limit and stick to it. Wrap up with a review of the conclusions reached or action to be taken.

Throw Out Something Every Day

Take a look around you every day, and discard the things you don't really need. Keep your waste basket well fed.

Keep Your Desk Clear

If you suffer from the stacked desk syndrome every time you look up from your work, you think of each pile on your desk as more work to be done, and your train of thought is interrupted. If you can't resist the temptation to stack at your work, at least move the piles out of sight, so they won't distract you.

Stop Procrastination

Procrastination, worrying and preoccupation with personal affairs or next day's work load are bigger time wasters. Some times we put off doing a job because the work entailed seems so massive. But getting started may be less painful than just thinking about it. Fear of failure sometimes leads us to avoid new situations in favour of doing over and over again those tasks we already do well. It's a sure way of limiting one's capabilities and usually leads to boredom.

Set Your Watch Fast

Achievement oriented individuals often set their watches a few minutes fast. It creates an extra sense of urgency. But don't become over concerned about getting a job done quickly. Sloppy results can mean having to do a job over.

Don't Plan to Work Overtime

Studies have shown that productivity declines rapidly after eight hours of work. Sometimes overtime is essential. But it can also become a habit, and an unproductive one. People who count on working overtime regularly to get their work done are not making the most effective use of their time during regular working hours.

Learn How to Delegate

This is one of the most obvious suggestions, but perhaps the most difficult to follow correctly. It's easy to fall into the trap of thinking something won't get done properly unless we do it ourselves.

Reward Yourself

After you have completed an important piece of work, give yourself a pat on the back. Take a few minutes to relax, and clear your mind before you launch the next one. Enjoy a sense of accomplishment.

If these principles are practised by managers, they will not only be able to manage their time effectively but will also enjoy it.

Generations of Time Management

The area of time management can be captured in a single phrase: organize and execute around priorities. That phrase represents the evolution of three generations of time management theory. In the area of time management each generation builds on the one before it. Each one moves us toward greater control of our lives. The first wave of generation could be characterized by notes and check lists, an effort to give some resemblance of recognition and inclusiveness to the many demands placed on our time and energy.

The second generation could be characterized by calendars and appointment books. This wave reflects an attempt to look ahead, to schedule events and activities in the future.

The third generation reflects the current time management field. It adds to those preceding generations the important idea of prioritization, of clarifying values, and of comparing the relative worth of activities based on their relationship to those values. In addition, it focuses on setting goals and targets towards which time and energy would be directed in harmony with values. It also includes the concept of daily planning, of making a specific plan to accomplish those goals and activities determined to be of greatest worth.

People however have begun to realise that 'efficient' scheduling and control of time are often counter productive. The efficiency focus creates expectations that clash with the opportunities to develop rich relationships, to meet human needs, and to enjoy spontaneous moments to be of greatest worth. As a result, many people have become turned off by time management programmes and planners that make them feel too scheduled, too restricted and reverting them to first or second generation techniques to preserve relationships, spontaneity and quality of life.

But there is an emerging fourth generation that is different in kind. It recognises that time management is really a misnomer – the challenge is not to manage time, but to manage ourselves. Satisfaction is a function of expectation as well as realization. Rather than focusing on things and time, fourth generation expectations focus on preserving and enhancing relationships and in accomplishing results. The essential focus of the fourth generation of management can be captured in the time management matrix (Exhibit 4) developed by Covey (1992)

According to Covey, basically, we spend time in one of four ways. The factors that define an activity are 'urgent' and 'important'. Urgent means it requires immediate attention. Urgent matters are usually visible. They press on attention. They are usually right in front of us. But so often they are unimportant. Importance, on the other hand, has to do with

Exhibit 4

The Time Management Matrix

	Urgent	*Not Urgent*
Important	I ACTIVITIES Crises Pressing problems Deadline driven projects	II ACTIVITIES Prevention Relationship building Recognising new opportunities Planning Recreation
Not Important	III ACTIVITIES Interruptions Mails, reports, calls Meetings Proximate, pressing matters Popular activities	IV ACTIVITIES Trivia, busy work Some mail Some phone calls Time wasters Pleasant activities

Source: Adapted from Covey (1992), 151.

results. It contributes to values, mission, and high priority goals. It is observed that we react to urgent matters irrespective of their importance level. We ignore important matters which are not urgent. Important matters that are not urgent, however, require more initiative, more proactively. We must act to seize opportunity, to make things happen. If we don't have a clear idea of what is important, of the results we desire in our lives, we are easily diverted into responding to the urgent.

Quadrant I in the matrix is both urgent and important. It deals with significant results that require immediate attention.

The activities in this quadrant are usually called 'crises' or 'problems'. Every one has such activities in daily life. It is commonly observed that Quadrant I consumes many managers. They are crisis managers, problem minded people, deadline-driven producers. As long as a manager focuses on Quadrant I, it keeps getting bigger and bigger until it dominates. A huge problem comes and knocks him down and he is wiped out. He struggles back up only to face another one that knocks him down and slams him to the ground. Some managers are literally beaten up by problems every day. The only relief they have is in escaping to the not important, not urgent activities of Quadrant IV. As a result of the study it is observed that 90 per cent of time of such managers is spent on Quadrant I and 10 per cent on Quadrant IV, with only negligible attention paid to other Quadrants. That is how people who manage their lives by crises live.

There are other managers who spend a great deal of time in 'urgent' but 'not important' activities (Quadrant III). They spend most of their time reacting to things that are urgent, assuming they are also important. But the reality is that the urgency of these matters is often based on the priorities and expectations of others. People who spend almost exclusively in Quadrants III and IV basically lead irresponsible lives.

Covey (1992) feels that effective people stay out of Quadrants III and IV and also shrink Quadrant I down to size spending more time in Quadrant II, which is the heart of effective personal management. It deals with things that are not urgent but are important. It deals with things like building relationships, writing a personal mission statement, long-range planning, exercising, preventive maintenance, preparation.

According to Peter Drucker, effective managers are not problem minded, they are opportunity minded. They feed opportunities and starve problems. They think preventively. They focus on the important but not urgent high leverage capacity building activities of Quadrant II.

Exhibit 5

Results of Concentrating on Activities Quadrant -Wise

Quadrant I	***Quadrant II***
Stress Burnout Crisis management Always putting out fires	Vision, perspective Balance Discipline Control Few crises
Quadrant III	***Quadrant IV***
Short-term focus Crisis management Reputation – chameleon character See goals and plans as worthless Feel victimized, out of control Shallow or broken relationships	Total irresponsibility Fired from jobs Dependent on others or institutions for basics

Source: Covey, (1992), 152-4

According to Covey, the results of focusing on activities falling under different Quadrants are eye opener. Managers who spend more time on urgent and important activities many a time they act is stress. They remain busy in managing the crises. Such managers unconsciously create crises and then try to manage. The managers who practice systematic planning, work preventively and devote much of their time on important but not urgent matters, they over a time become effective managers. The managers who escape to urgent but not important activities they are basically victim of undertaking unproductive time killing tasks. The managers who are busy with neither urgent nor important activities, and simply pass the time, they behave irresponsibly and become liability to the organisation (Exhibit 5). Thus, the study corroborates the observation of many earlier research studies that managers who commit more time on important but not urgent activities, are highly effective.

The managers who do thinking and systematic planning of their activities on the basis of 'importance' and not always according to 'urgency' devote much of their time on preventive matters which have long- term effectiveness. They prioritize their activities and work in a 'win-win' situation. In result they face little crisis. It has been proved that highly effective and successful managers world over spend about 70 per cent of their time in activities that are important and not urgent. (Covey: 1992) Importance is concerned with values, perspective, prevention and discipline, while urgency is linked with the time. It is irony that many public sector managers behave like bureaucrats working in a hierarchical organisation. Their main objective is to follow the boss and adhere to rules and regulations. They lack initiative. Most of the managers keep low profile, pass the time and keep eye always on their elevation. They keep away from planning and prioritising.

For years people have been keeping track of meetings, appointments, telephone calls and unfinished work by using daily planning books – Day Timers, Day Runners, File Fixers, and Franklin Planners. These personal organizers have been wonderful productivity improvement tools. They have helped us set our priorities, organise and coordinate our important long-term project, keep track of our delegated work, and establish and set goals. We have also used them to get down notes or background information about our business meetings and phone conservations, keep track of miscellaneous ideas and thoughts.

In this backdrop, the managers were asked as to whether they use any mechanism to record utilisation of their time. They were unanimous that there is no time planning for any activity in general. They are found having no data about the use of their time. But they have instruments to record the works to be done during the day (Table 2.6). In office, all the managers have two sets of diaries or engagement pads – one with him and other with his personal staff (secretary). The important meetings and other engagements are recorded by the secretary in both the diaries. Some times manager himself makes a note in his diary. The secretary is directed to however remind the manager in many cases about the engagements.

Some managers are found using loose papers or small pocket diary to note the activities related to household chores. Some claims to have strong memory, hence every thing is stored in their mind. A few dynamic managers especially in private sector use palm computer for storing important informations including engagements. A few have electronic diary, but to store specifically important phone numbers. It is surprising that the engagements and other important activities of managers in public sector are managed by secretaries. Higher the level, more dependence on personal staff, is the real life story in public sector. The situation is some what different in private sector.

It is thus clear that most Indian managers are in first and second generation of time management only, moreso, not in a planned way but because of certain compulsions. They are trained to maintain detail of engagements just not to cut a sorry face before their bosses. In turn, private secretaries are much concerned about engagements of their boss. This system was introduced in view of the diverse over-commitment of administrators in olden days, but today having a large contingent of personal staff has become of a symbol of status in official hierarchy rather than a necessity. It demands a rethinking on restructuring the public sector enterprises, which are overstaffed and have been converted into haven of inefficient people in the name of welfare and social commitment.

Table 2.6
Mechanism Used for Planning the Time Instruments

Instruments	*Users* (Percentage Distribution)
Engagement Pads/Diaries	55.00
Pocket diaries	10.00
Electronic Planner/Diary	15.00
Memory	10.00
Palm top Computer	5.00
Nothing/Others (slips)	5.00
Total	**100.00**

As regards classifying their activities as important and urgent, it is surprising that managers do favour such classification and claim sometimes to group activities but their list of tasks is disrupted by the (urgent) orders received from the boss. The orders of the seniors or top management have to be complied with on priority basis. The urgency hammers importance, because urgency is related to time and importance to substance. For want of systematic planning urgency prevails in the public sector organisations most of the time. This clearly shows the lack of planning by managers. There is every scope to receive urgent matters from the top boss, but the whole time structure should not be allowed to collapse. The managers should plan their tasks in such a way that there remains a cushion to urgent matters. Such a situation warrants systematic planning by managers.

The officials were furnished a list of activities concerning to their job responsibilities and were requested to prioritise on the basis of time devoted by them. The analysis (Table 2.7) reveals that the basic activities like 'planning', 'developing', and 'motivating' are at the lowest ebb of the managers. Activities reflecting authority (directing, supervising) are at the comparatively upper ladder. The activities totally unproductive (meetings, mails, telephone calls) snatch a good part of the manager's time. Surprisingly about one-third of the working hours of a manager are generally spent on fighting the crises and the pressing problems before the organisation. Such a situation can be avoided if managers give more time to preventive activities instead of maintenance activities. Crisis at rare occasions may be welcomed but management by crisis

Table 2.7
Time Devoted by Managers on Major Activities

Nature of Activities	*Time devoted (Percentage Distribution)*
Planning	3.00
Directing	5.00
Supervising	7.00
Developing	5.00
Motivating	3.00
Meetings	15.00
Mails	10.00
Telephone calls	10.00
Pressing problems	15.00
Crises	20.00
Others	7.00
Total	**100.00**

may not be termed a very good proposition. The managers should avoid the recurrence of such situations.

If fitted into the Time Management Matrix developed by Management Guru Stephen R. Covey majority of the managers are found spending lot of time in Quadrants I, III and IV. The activities falling under Quadrant II often fail to attract their attention,whereas the approach should be in reverse direction. If more time is devoted to activities belonging to Quadrant II (promotive and preventing measures), the efficiency and effectiveness of the individual as well as the organisation will undoubtedly increase tremendously. But only the managers are not responsible for this situation. The whole working culture of public sector needs to be changed. Top management officials keep the middle managers at tenterhook. Merit is not the criterion for getting top positions in public sector. Simultaneously, lower level officials are not adaptive. The middle level managers thus avoid any initiative because it may lead to confrontation at both the end. In such a working environment, managers prefer to go by management by crises. There is very little scope for prevention values, and substance.

The chapter thus can be concluded with a short remark that if HRD managers working with public sector enterprises conceive idea of time management as life management, no doubt their effectiveness will increase tremendously and quality of their life will better. The managers should prepare a personal mission, set some agenda for their official as well as personal life, prepare a perspective plan, set their priorities and work in a win-win situation. Their efficiency will certainly improve tremendously and they will become effective managers in office and successful individual in personal life.

References

Bajaj, B.L. (1998), Time Management, Prashasnika, XXV (1), January-June

Thomas, Philip R. with K.R. Martin (1991), Getting Competitive: Middle Managers and the cycle time ethic, Mc Graw Hill, Inc., New York.

Thomas, Philip R. (1989), Competitiveness through Total Cycle Time, Mc Graw Hill, New York

Hibbard, Janet G. and Landrum, Robert K. (1978), How to Fight Time and Win, Personnel Journal, May

Mackenzie, R. Alec and Kau, Dennis le (1975), Take a Quite Hour....For Time to Think and Plan, American Society for Training Directors, June

Rotenbury, Harry C.(1978), Time Management and Communication, Management World, September

Rotenbury, Harry C. (1979), Time Management Scheduling, Management World, May

The Royal Bank of Canada, Monthly Letter, Why Procrastinate, 40 (9), 52

Bensahel, Jane G. (1979), Getting the Best out of Your Time, International Management, June, 60

Porter, W. Thomas Jr. (1978), Time and Self Management, Journal of Accountancy, June, 58

Mackenzie, R. Alec (1975), New Time Management Methods for You and Your Staff, Dartnell, Chicago

Drucker, Peter F. (1964-70), Drucker on Management, Management Pub. Ltd., London

Moore, Leo B. (1968), Management Time, Industrial Management Review, Spring, 77-85

Meier, Richard L. (1959), Human Time Allocation: A Basis for Social Accounts, Journal of the American Institute of Planners, 25, 27-33

Nakanishi, Naomichi (1963), Report on the How –Do-People- Spend-Their Time Survey: An Analysis of Livelihood Time of the Japanese, NHK Radio and T.V. Culture Research Institute, Tokyo

Sorokin, P.A. and Berger, C.Q. (1939), Time Budgets of Human Behaviour, Harvard University Press, Cambridge, Mass.

Szalai, Alexander (1966), Trends in Comparative Time Budget Research, American Behavioural Scientist, 9(9), 3-8

United Nations Educational, Scientific and Cultural Organisation (1966), The Multinational Comparative Time Budget Research Project, European Coordination Centre for Research and Documentation in Social Sciences, Vienna

Adair, John and Allen, Melanie (2003), Time Management and Personal Development, Viva Books, New Delhi

Soule, G. (1955), Time for Living, Viking Press, New York

Adcock, Robert L. (1970), The Management Process: A Preliminary Statement of its Functions and Principles and a Survey of their Use, unpublished Master's Thesis, School of Business, Florida State University

Saxena, Shailendra (2000), Integrated Time Management, Hindustan Times, New Delhi, May 18

Lakein, Alan (1973), How to Get Control of Your Time and Your Life, Signet, New York

Mathur, K.M. (1993), Towards Effective Management (Pathways to Excellence), Gyan, New Delhi, 89-110

Sharma, Rajiv (1981), Time Management, unpublished mimeo, Training Material, Institute of Public Administration, Lucknow University

Covey, Stephen R. (1992), The Seven Habits of Highly Effective People, Simon & Schuster, London

Robinson, John P. and Godbey, Geoffrey (1997), Time for Life:,The Surprising Ways Americans Use Their Time, Pennsylvania University Press, Park

Robinson, John P. (1977), How Americans Use Time: A Social Psychological Analysis of Everyday Behavior, Praeger, New York

Sharp, Clifford (1981), The Economics of Time, John Wiley & Sons, New York

Bell, Daniel (1973), The Coming of Post-Industrial Society: A venture in Social Forecasting, Basic Books, New York

Douglass, Merrill E. (1975), Creative use of Time, The Personnel Administrator, October

Robbins (1945), as quoted in Sharp, C. (1981), The Economics of Time, John Wiley & Sons, New York, 4

Linder (1970), as quoted in Robinson, J.P. (1977), How Americans Use Time: A Social Psychological Analysis of Everyday Behavior, Praeger, New York

3

Managing Personal Development

Available time is equal for every one, irrespective of the fact whether one is high or low, rich or poor. Twenty four hours a day are twenty four hours for every one. Here, law of socialism operates perfectly well. Hence, one's success depends upon effective management of one's time.

Time Management is Life Management

Soul of all managements, time management, indeed is the management of life. Time is just an image of eternity, said Plato. We can feel it but neither touch it nor catch it and nor preserve it for future use. Money, on the other hand, can be saved today and used tomorrow but time cannot be thus preserved, and therefore, carried much more importance than money and hence obviously is most precious. Time is synonym of life in a sense and some wish to call it currency of life. Einstein termed it as fourth dimension. Indians recognised importance of time as an independent entity/dimension from time immemorial. (Bajaj: 1998)

Douglass (1975) emphasizes that "Learning to control your time means changing some of your time habits. But you can't change time habits until you first know what those habits are." Our character basically is a composite of our habits. Habits are powerful factors in our lives. Because they are consistent, often unconscious patterns, they constantly, daily, express our character and produce our effectiveness. Habit may be defined as the interaction of knowledge, skill and desire as depicted in Exhibit 6. (Covey: 1992:4)

Exhibit 6
Interaction between Habits, Knowledge, Skill and Desire

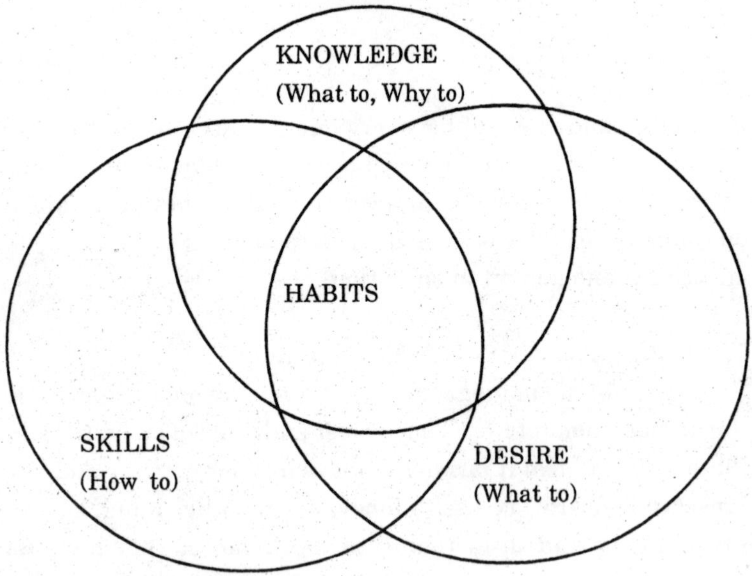

Source: Adapted from Covey, 1992, 4

A Cold Look

According to experts, setting of goals is necessary to control time and life. It is important to be pursuing the right personal goals. (Hibbard & Landrum: 1978:256) Managers should plan the time by setting goals divided into long-term and short-term objectives. They should determine the time to devote to each proposed of the goal set. (Mathur: 1993:90)

After understanding how a manager is using his time, the next step is to examine his time utilisation vis-à-vis his life objectives. Most people are so concerned about 'doing things right' that they rarely pause to consider whether they are doing the 'right things'. The day-to-day running around may contribute nothing towards life objectives and thus may not be the right things to do. This involves a 'cold look' at one's life style asking two basic questions: (a) where does he want to go? (b) where is he going now?

This analysis should focus on two aspects: (1) how much time is spent on tasks that are routine in nature and which do not lead to personal development; and (2) how much time is 'invested' on tasks that are challenging and innovative and thus lead to personal development over a period of time. The goal of life should be identified and personal development should be directed towards these goals.

As regards setting of the personal goals by the HRD Managers covered under the study, the responses were very vague and general. The respondents were not clear about the goals of their life. (Table 3.1)

It is a sad state of affairs that getting job for most of the managers was the main goal and now they seem satisfied with whatever they have achieved in life. Now, their only worry is the career of children and social security and recognition. In Indian situation where unemployment is rampant, getting a job is the sole aim.

The managers however were deemed somewhat confused with goal, aim, objectives. Despite all ambiguity, every human being has goal to achieve in life. The managers while setting the personal goals compatible to organisational objectives have to take into consideration many factors including the environment in which organisation works. Most of the managers (middle aged) did not have set any personal goal. After having finished study they wanted a job to earn their livelihood and they are satisfied on this count. Now, at the advance age, they are totally concerned with the career of their children, their leading a happy married life, getting a good job.

Table 3.1
Goal Setting by Managers

(Percentage Distribution)

Factors	*YES*		*No*	*Total*
	Great Extent	Some Extent		
Managers have set the personal goals	50	30	20	100
They have determined				
a) long term objectives	40	30	30	100
b) short-term objectives	60	20	20	100
They have allotted time to each goal	20	40	40	100

Managers have no specific personal goals in life. They were found some what confused with organisational goals. Every enterprise has its goal set, and the managers have to perform the tasks assigned to them. Many of them were found having been failed in assimilating their personal objectives into organisational objectives. Some times their personal objectives overtake organisational ones, as they feel their behaviour in no way affects the organisation. Their attitude needs to be changed through development efforts and making the managers 'organisation man'.

It was observed that managers were concerned only to finish the tasks for which they are responsible. They never bother about others. They believe in doing things right and never give a thought to do right things. They were not clear about 'right things' or 'doing things rightly'. Whatever they do, that is their assigned work and there is no scope to see whether it is right or wrong. They do it rightly, that is their main aim. Their attempt all the time remains to adhere to the rules and regulations.

Managerial Excellence

Organisational effectiveness is defined situationally, of course. The right timing, the right national mood, the 'hot' new product, the untapped demand for a social service, the charisma of its leaders, the special skills and political acumen of its top executive, lucky events in its environment, all play a part in the health and development of any enterprise. But through all the ups and downs, through all the lucky and unlucky changes in the environment, with all the lucky and unlucky guesses about what to do, one variable stands out as most instrumental in organisational effectiveness. That variable is managerial performance, the ability of a small group of key individuals to chart a course and to guide the efforts of others along it. Managerial performance always forms a key element of an organisation's effectiveness. (Albrecht: 1978)

The organisations interact with a number of environments. The managers have to work for their effectiveness in tune to the organisational culture and internal and external environments. The effectiveness of a manager depends upon successful interactions with the environments. (Exhibit 7) For the purpose, managers have to develop a composite personality equipped to make the interactions positive. The managers have to plan their development compatible to the changing varied environments. In addition, managers are citizen as well.

Exhibit 7
The Organisation Interacts with Variety of Environments

Source: Adapted from Albrecht, 1978, 1

They should be aware of the internal environment and external environments. Their success as a manager and also as a citizen depends upon the extent of mutual interactions amongst environments established by them.

The post-liberalised economy is posing many additional challenges before the Indian public sector and its managers, especially HRD Managers. The emerging era of competitiveness and a turn around in form of right sizing of public sector enterprises, the managers have to interact with multi-national companies which produce quality products with less investment comparatively in less time.

Personal Competence

Personal competence is regarded as the foundation of personal effectiveness and flexible management. To be able to perform effectively, managers need to bring a level of personal competence to their jobs. Personal competencies are transferable and reflect the skills needed for the process of management. Key roles in management are:

- Managing operations
- Managing finance
- Managing people
- Managing information

These key managerial roles are broken down in specific units of competence. The key areas stay the same while the units of competence vary in range and scope with each level of management. The Model of Personal Competence as developed by Adair and Allen, on the other hand, is the same for all levels of management.

The HRD Managers covered under the study were asked to assess themselves and reveal the extent of their excellence and competence. For the purpose they were given a number of variables and were requested to assess them. The responses (Table 3.2) are self explanatory. The managers find themselves fully competent. It seems that the long experience of managers and stereotype organisational functioning keep every manager in maintaining the performance level. There is no yardstick to adjudge the level of competence of managers.

There is no mechanism to assess their potential. However, the long rich experience in the field and the academic background have placed them to that level of satisfaction. They are always conscious about their performance report, which

The Personal Competence Model

Clusters of Personal Competence	*Dimensions of Personal Competence*
1. Planning to optimize the achievement of results	• Showing concern for excellence • Setting and prioritising objectives • Monitoring and responding to actual against planned activities
2. Managing others to optimize results	• Showing sensitivity to the needs of others • Relating to others • Obtaining the commitment of others • Presenting oneself positively to others
3. Managing oneself to optimize results	• Showing self confidence and personal drive • Managing personal emotions and stress • Managing personal learning and development
4. Using intellect to optimize results	• Collecting and organising information • Identifying and applying concepts • Taking decisions

Source: Adapted from Adair & Allen (2003), 77-8

lacks objectivity. The fixed routine and rigid rules and regulations hinder dynamism and innovation in their working. The managers in general are involved in maintenance of their performance rather than in adventuring initiatives and face danger. Every manager is found working safe. They lack initiative in general and prefer doing things rightly. Most of them are found neither conscious about their development nor concerned to the development of their subordinates. This may be because of their age. Such an approach hampers their sincerity and effectiveness.

Surprisingly, managers in general lack role clarity. They are somewhat ignorant of the developmental approach hidden in HRD technique. They fail to differentiate traditional personnel functions with HRD functions. The managers are not much involved in enriching the jobs, to make the tasks interesting. They have neither any mission for their own development nor any initiative for developing their subordinates. Their supervision lacks development approach. Managers believe in using authority rather than persuasion to motivate the subordinates and develop them.

There is a need to orient the managers to their development needs. Not only have the managers, officials at all levels need proper and periodical development orientation. The higher officials should appreciate the development initiatives taken by managers and the officials at operational level should adapt themselves with the changing development scenario. The public sector should formulate a training policy and all the officials should be imparted training. The job responsibilities at every position be clearly earmarked and the managers should make every effort to enrich the job. The job rotation amongst officials is practised to create interest. The techniques of HRD are adopted in proper perspective.

Personal Sense of Time

Time is money. It is a limited and valuable resource, but it is actually more precious and cannot be stored. Time is our life as measured out in years, months, days, hours, minutes and seconds. One cannot control time in the sense of stopping it, slowing it down or speeding it up. But one can apply it economically to the tasks he has to accomplish. (Adair & Allen: 2003:33)

Time budgeting is one exercise whereby managers can plan and allocate segments of time available for various activities over a period projecting into the future. This time allocation

Table 3.2

Level of Excellence& Competence

Variables	*Most Extent*	*Great Extent*	*Some Extent*	*Normal*	*Average*	*Fair*	*Total*
Aware of Organisation's Objectives	70	20	5	5	-	-	100
Knowledge of working of the organisation	60	20	10	7	3	-	100
Role clarity	50	25	10	5	7	3	100
Enriching the job	40	20	10	15	10	5	100
Developing subordinates	25	20	15	10	20	10	100
Motivating employees	30	20	20	10	15	5	100
Well acquainted with latest techniques in the field	27	25	15	13	10	10	100
Understanding subordinates' competence level	20	30	20	10	15	5	100
Ccrdiality with peers	60	20	10	5	3	2	100
Supervision development oriented	20	30	20	15	10	5	100
Encourage subordinates	25	35	20	10	8	2	100
Working problems solved immediately	40	30	20	10	-	-	100
Interpersonal relations harmonious	60	25	10	5	-	-	100
Team working facilitating	50	20	10	10	5	5	100

must be reviewed from time to time. A comprehensive time budgeting will cover all activities affecting his life – short term and long term. (Kharb : 2003:197)

Developing a personal sense of time includes developing a personal sense of the value of other people's time. We must have a distinct view of our life, career or business. Our time plan therefore must encompass the entire life. Job, family, friends, health and entertainment are all essential parts of life. Judicious allocation of time for all these activities helps us lead a balanced life.

It was thought pertinent to assess the level of personal sense of time amongst the managers. A number of indicators were provided and their responses were fetched. Although the managers extrovertly reflectd their personal sense of time (Table 3.3), the observations reveal otherwise. They are found indulging in long gossiping sessions. In the name of meetings they spend hours. They keep visitors, subordinates waiting for

Table 3.3
Level of Personal Sense of Time

(Percentage Distribution)

Indicators	*Yes*	*No*	*Total*
Managers treat time as a thing to manage	50	50	100
They manage time - at office	95	5	100
- at home	70	30	
They care for time of – Superiors	90	10	100
- Subordinates	60	40	
They make distinction between office and personal time	70	30	100
They allocate time for each activity	20	80	100
They link time with			
- personal development	60	40	100
- leading a balanced life	50	50	100
- health	60	40	100
- family	75	25	100

nothing. Time taken in responding is a symbol of level. The easily accessible and approachable manager is treated not on high pedestal amongst his peers. A little number of managers were found having some sense of time. Most managers (especially at the advanced age) have no concern to the time. Time comes, time passes, this is their routine. Some training orientation towards managing time may create some sense amongst the managers.

Objective Setting and Action Planning

The journey of self development does not follow a straight road. It is a life long process. Self development is a journey not a destination. Development objectives should be: Specific, Measurable, Agreed, Realistic, Time bound, Evaluated, Reviewed, Strategic, Meaningful, Attainable, Rewarding, Team Building, and Empowering. (Adair & Allen: 2003:117-123)

The long journey of personal development begins with a simple step. A manager will never achieve an objective if he does not break it down into manageable steps. Each day should see him and his team some steps nearer to his projected and desired results.

To become successful today managers should become more productive, efficient and effective and not just busy. When productivity increases, the quality of work improves, one gets things done on time, and best of all, he accomplishes more tasks with less effort. If he wants to learn how to manage his time better, he has got to become aware of how he is spending his time during a typical business day. His goal should not be to have nice, neat, orderly desk. The desk is secondary. His goal is to get organised so that he can convert time that's wasted during the course of normal business day any time that can be used more efficiently and effectively. (Mayer: 1995:3-12)

It is an essential discipline to compile a programme for the day. In return managers gain a sense of control, direction and freedom which is other wise impossible. They should set time limits for all tasks and get of into the way of always estimating the amount of time required to do each job and then should establish priorities. A priority is composed of two elements in various mixtures: urgency and importance. If they have worked according to their sense of priorities they will have done the important jobs, and that is what managing their time all is about.

Managers should not leave day planning to the last minute. They should plan their day outline a week ahead and in detail on the eve of it. A manager should firmly decide when he will complete the one or two really important tasks of the day and block some time out to deal with these. He should consider when he will do the remaining tasks and allot time accordingly.

A review can establish whether or not time budget of manager was realistic in the first place. If it was, then the problem lies in the area of execution. The most common reason for failing to accomplish is found interruptions. To counter them, he must learn to use one of the shortest and most time saving words 'No'. But one should remember to 'be ruthless with time – gracious with people'. (Adair & Allen: 2003: 34) He should learn to say 'no'; otherwise he will become merely the servant to the priorities of others. It is easy to become efficient without becoming odious. His practice of time management should enable him to contribute more to society and to others, and not act as their judge.

A manager should make the best use of his time because it has been established by research that 20 per cent of time produces 80 per cent of high quality output.(Covey:1992) Hence he should regularly programme his day in such a way so that best time is given to the highest grade activities, such as strategic thinking.

If a manager would like to improve his daily productivity and take control of all of his daily activities, his telephone calls, to-dos, meetings and appointments, he may start using a contact manager and put his daily planner inside his computer. The whole idea of using a computer is to help him get more work done in less time. And with a contact manager he can coordinate the basic components of his planner with single software programme. (Mayer: 1995:47)

Time is not in our control. Good or bad days and years will pass, irrespective of our desire and deeds. We cannot stop or store time for later use. The entire world's wealth cannot buy us an extra second. But we can organise our self in a way that will entice good times and repel bad times. Good times will get over faster if we do nothing; bad ones will take longer time for inactive people. Conversely, if we launch our self whole heartedly in purposeful activities, good time will last and bad ones disappear. (Kharb: 2003:194)

In respect of managers having set some objectives, the responses are totally ambiguous. (Table 3.4) The managers are little conscious about self development but they are much concerned about their elevation in hierarchy. Their promotion is development for them. Their main objective is to get promoted to higher posts. They do plan the day but urgency often derails their plan. Thus their plan is totally adhoc and has no systematic characteristic.

Many managers feel that there is no scope for setting objectives and identify priority works as everything is done in a pre-determined manner and of course orders from the top are most urgent. The managers are found having little idea about their best time, but they plan serious works in the beginning of the day. Most of the managers have personal computers, but their computers have replaced the typewriters. They have no contact manager system but see no scope for any such software in near future. Since they don't plan and allocate time for each and every activity, there are no mechanisms to assess the time saving. The managers however feel 'free time' as a saved time and they spend their 'free time' generally in unproductive activities. Thus everything related to time is in mess and the organisations are being run on the bureaucratic line, managers being the key administrators.

Making Use of Committed Time

Time comes in different guises. Basically at work there is 'discretionary time', the time which a manager can choose to spend as he will – and 'committed time'. Committed time is time that is booked for one reason or another. However, if a manager is alert he may find portions of it which are actually free time. Daily routines are in effect committed time. Committed time is a time which is fixed and the managers have to comply with the requirements of that time. It is basically a time for which managers are employed. It is fixed generally at eight hours in public sector enterprises. Committed time is paid time because managers are paid for that period.

Table 3.4
Setting Objectives and Planning

(Percentage Distribution)

Indicators	*Great Extent*	*Some Extent*	*Not*	*No Scope*	*Total*
Conscious about self development	70	30	-	-	100
Set development objectives	30	20	30	20	100
Objectives are					
- specific	50	30	20	-	100
- realistic	70	30	-	-	100
- time bound	20	40	30	10	100
- reviewed	10	20	65	5	100
- attainable	60	30	-	10	100
- development oriented	70	20	-	10	100
- leading to team working	50	30	10	10	100

(Contd.)

(Contd. Table 3.4)

Indicators	*Great Extent*	*Some Extent*	*Not*	*No Scope*	*Total*
Activities divided in steps	50	20	10	20	100
Goal at job:					
- to have nice, clear desk	20	30	50	-	100
- get organised	30	25	25	20	100
- a combination of both	70	30	-	-	100
Have a programme for the day	60	20	10	10	100
They set priorities on the basis of					
- urgency	70	20	-	10	100
- importance	40	30	-	30	100
- combination of both	50	30	10	10	100
- no priorities set	40	30	10	20	100
Have identified best time	40	20	20	20	100
Managers have personal computers	Yes				80
	No				20
Managers have a contact manager	Yes				-
	No				100
Managers do save time	Yes				50
	No				30
	Less time				20
Saved time is spent					
- on other activities					60
- on planning /thinking					10
- on meetings					25
- just pass on					5

The HRD Managers expressed to be over busy during the day. Some of them confessed to spend some time on personal works as the works can be completed during the day and they remain at office. Such works included attending of schools of children, visiting for health check up or any other emergency. In reality, however, many personal works of managers are got done by subordinates during committed hours. Overstaffing and less work and degrading values in life have made such practices justifiable.

There should be division of works and job responsibilities be fixed for better use of time. Every one from top to bottom should be encouraged to make best use of his committed time. It is surprising that managers seldom give any value to their time. In case of any payment to be made, hourly rates are derived but in no other case any price is added to time. Every second of committed time has some value and its loss directly affects productivity. Every second of committed hours has multiplier effect on overall performance of enterprise. Hence, time must be used effectively and productively.

Table 3.5
Use of Committed Time

(Percentage Distribution)

Indicators	*Yes*	*No*	*Not Aware*	*No Response*	*Total*
Whether managers classify time as committed time, free time, discretionary time, personal time	30	20	40	10	100
Making best use of committed (working) time	85	10	-	05	100
They have free time out of committed time	25	60	-	15	100
Are they overburdened	75	10	-	15	100
They occasionally do personal work during routine time	15	80	-	5	100

Further it was a major concern to know whether managers plan their day in advance. The officials in this connection confined them to divulge information about their working hours only. Hence, it was attempted to have the extent of their committed hours. It is clear (Table 3.6) that working hours differ. Public sector enterprises have eight hours of routine day while private sector in many fields differs in this regard. In some enterprises routine hours are ten. A few have six hours as well.

Table 3.6

Extent of Committed Hours

Working Hours	*Responses(PercentageDistribution)*
6	5
8	85
10	10
Total	100

On further probing, managers expressed spending a large portion of their working time in performing their normal professional works (Table 3.7). However, the managers could not elaborate the nature and content of their normal tasks. It seems to be routine work. The analysis reveals that a large part of their committed hours is eaten away by routine works. It may be that every work done by managers is generally of routine nature. They have very little scope for innovations.

Table 3.7

Time Spent on Normal Professional Works

Period (hours)	*Response level (Percentage Distribution)*
3	
4	50
5	15
6	30
7	05
Total	100

The managers were further requested to disclose the way they spend their committed hours. The pattern of spending working hours by managers is depicted in Table 3.8.

The analysis (Table 3.8) highlights that the managers spend six hours per week on travel to office and back to home. Many a time managers travel during day hours as well. Most of the managers use official car, hence their travel time is totally free time. Many managers read newspapers and magazines during travel time. Some makes calls, mostly personal. About one-sixth of managers' time every week is used on getting feedback from subordinates and giving feedback to their boss. The managers were not quite clear about the contents of feedback but it seems the time is used for stock taking of the human affairs and issues related to

Table 3.8

Pattern of Use of Committed Hours

(Average time spent out of 8 hours)

Activities	*Time spent per day (minutes)*	*Time spent per week (hrs)*	*Proportion to total Working hours (6 days) (%)*
Travel (both ways)	60	6.0	*
Getting feedback (team meeting)	45	4.5	9.37
Taking round	30	3.0	6.25
Briefing to boss	30	3.0	6.25
Telephones	45	4.5	9.37
Visitors	30	3.0	6.25
Meetings	90	9.0	18.75
Desk work	90	9.0	18.75
Thinking/Planning	45	4.5	9.37
Rest/Break	30	3.0	6.25
Other works (not specified)	45	4.5	9.37
Total	480	48.0	

*Travel time not included in analysis.

formal meetings, it becomes disastrous. More than one-fifth of office hours are spent on meetings alone. Some times these meetings are held to firefighting and managing the crises, disputes and industrial unrests. The creation of a separate employees' grievance redressal cell may help to get rid of such meetings to a great extent. Further, every petty issue of personnel be taken care of and addressed fairly before it takes a bad turn and becomes a major issue.

A meagre time is used by managers on thinking including planning. In public sector enterprises everything is pre-determined by the top management under the overall policy framework formulated by the government, the managers are left with planning related only to operational issues. They are confined to planning related to petty matters. They are responsible for operating in the right earnest. A little amount of time is spent by managers on vending. It is realistic in case of HRD Managers who are not supposed to visit production centres. Managers spend about one-sixth of their working hours on telephone calls and attending visitors. Every manager in public sector is duty bound to allot some time for public but HRD Managers have little concern with the public. The time spent on visitors may be on attending internal visitors or personal visitors. A good part of managers' time is used (wasted) in paper work, in the form of letters, memos, and periodical reports etc. which have no productive value. Although rest period is prescribed, in real sense, more time is spent on this unproductive activity.

It is observed that individual manager's objectives and goals are not specifically defined. They claim to discharge the assigned works efficiently. The effectiveness of their time is neither examined nor do the managers have any concern about the same. Things are quite different in private sector units. Their managers have definite role to play. Their goals and objectives are clearly framed and performance is measured daily in the form of productivity. The managers working in public sector have a different mindset than that of their counterparts in the other sector. The managers engaged with public sector some how behave like 'boss' and they seldom form themselves a part of their units (team) because they are not oriented to link themselves with the overall productivity of the enterprise.

Every manager works in isolation. They may be efficient in their respective sectors but organisational effectiveness (cumulative effectiveness) is less than the total sum. The public sector managers, therefore need to inculcate and follow a corporate culture much suited to the emerging competitive market.

Management Time

It is generally observed that managers typically run out of time while their subordinates typically run out of work. Management time relates to the interaction between managers and their bosses, their peers and their subordinates. Oncken and Wass (1999) discuss three kinds of management time: Boss-imposed time, System-imposed time and Self-imposed time. Boss-imposed time is used to accomplish those activities that the boss requires and that the manager cannot disregard without direct and swift penalty. System-imposed time is used to accommodate requests from peers for active support. Neglecting these requests will also result in penalties, though not always as direct or swift. Self-imposed time is used to do those things that the manager originates or agrees to do. A certain portion of this kind of time, however, will be taken by subordinates and is called subordinate-imposed time. The remaining portion will be the manager's own and is called discretionary time. Self-imposed time is not subject to penalty since neither the boss nor the system can discipline the manager for not doing what they didn't know he had intended to do in the first place.

To accommodate those demands managers need to control the timing and the content of what they do. Since what their boss and the system impose on them is subject to penalty, managers cannot temper with those requirements. Thus their self-imposed time becomes their major area of concern. Managers should try to increase the discretionary component of their self-imposed time by minimizing or doing away with the subordinate components. They will then use the added increment to get better control over their boss-imposed and system-imposed activities.

During the study, the managers were asked as to how they behave with the above three times. All the managers were unanimous that they are obliged at all the time to go by the boss-imposed time. They have no choice. The system-imposed time is at the second ladder while prioritising their works. The self-imposed time is very limited. Most of the times at office are spent while going by the boss-imposed and system-imposed times. A portion of system-imposed time may be converted into self-imposed time by adopting the day planning. The extent of self-imposed time depends upon planning the time. Unfortunately, most of the managers fight with the boss-imposed and system-imposed times. The situation requires a thoughtful and realistic time planning by the managers.

Table 3.9
Treating Management Time

Management Time	*First Preference*	*Second Preference*	*Third Preference*	*Total*
Boss-imposed Time	95	5	-	100
System-imposed Time	20	70	10	100
Self-imposed Time	20	15	65	100

There are five degrees of initiative that the managers can exercise in relation to the boss and to the system: wait until told (lowest initiative), as what to do, recommend, then take resulting action, act but advise at once, and act on own, then routinely report (highest initiative). (Oncken & Wass: 1999: 184) Clearly, the manager should be professional enough not to indulge in first two initiatives in relation to either to the boss or to the system. A manager who uses first initiative has no imposed time. The manager who uses second initiative has control over the timing but not over the content. Last three initiatives leave the manager in control of both, with the greatest amount of control being exercised at last level.

In relation to subordinates, the manager's job is two fold. First, to outlaw the use of first and second initiatives, thus giving subordinates no choice but to learn. Second, to see that for each problem there is an agreed upon level of initiative assigned to it, in addition to an agreed upon time and place for the next manager-subordinate meeting.

Table 3.10
Initiatives Adopted by Managers

(Percentage Distribution)

Initiatives	*Great Extent*	*Some Extent*	*Not*	*Total*
Wait until told	55	25	10	100
Ask what to do	40	30	30	100
Take resulting action	20	25	55	100
Act on own	10	30	60	100
Reporting	60	35	5	100

The HRD Managers covered under the study were asked to identify the initiatives taken by them in relation to three types of management time, which combinedly make committed hours. It is clear from the analysis (Table 3.10) that most of the managers use initiative one and two. In the hierarchical organisations like public sector enterprises, managers are obliged to carry out the directives of the top management. There is little scope for own initiative. Reporting to boss is necessary otherwise it may attract adverse action. Such a state of affairs corroborates the large portion of committed time used by managers in routine works.

Organising Office Work

Paper work and interruptions are the factors which affect time efficiency and effectiveness framework. Although most text books say that one should refuse to be interrupted, we all know in practice that it often makes sense to accept the interruptions. But we must control it. We should give people full attention and listen to them well. A manager should be firm but friendly and helpful and let them not go away empty handed if he can avoid it. (Adair & Allen: 2003)

Priorities navigate a manager properly and smoothly to his destination. He remains focused on the mission, with all resources appropriately mobilised. In the absence of 'priorities', he not only dissipated his time and resources but also run the risk of failing to achieve his targets. Technology has made working a smarter activity in three ways: it saves time, money and space, enhances the speed and productivity of an employee and is convenient. The concept of smart office includes the efficient and optimum utilisation of resources to produce smart and better results. The three components that make for a smart office are networking, wireless technology and Blue tooth. The government since recent past has been emphasising on computerization of office working. It has been however observed that many public enterprises are still far behind in this direction.

In Indian public sector office work is maintained by the subordinates. The piles of papers are kept by the lower level staff. The public sector organisations function on the pattern prescribed by top management. Every where there is a fixed system and rules and regulations have been framed either by the government or the management board and managers have to follow them unfailingly. Any lapse on their part may invite trouble. In the rigid system there is very little scope for innovation. The managers adopt some local arrangements for weeding out unnecessary old papers. Works to subordinates are allocated by them but no major organisational changes in office working can be introduced by managers themselves.

As regards attending visitors, every manager has some time fixed exclusively for the visitors. Visitors are usually never treated as interrupter. All the phone calls incoming and outgoing are managed by the personal staff or secretary of the manager. Most of the committed hours are eaten away by lay and frequent meetings. Higher the level of officials, more number of meetings, is the general phenomenon in Indian offices. The organisations are run on meetings only. Meeting, talking all the time, but less work, this is the general pattern of functioning in public sector organisations.

Managers are mostly flooded with papers. Sometimes they are lost in the piles of papers. The managers should attempt to reduce the paper works. All the papers are not important and worth keeping indefinitely. The weeding out of papers should be done periodically. The desk should be kept neat and clean so that unnecessary papers piled on the desk do not distract managers from important serious working. It is surprising that managers are putting in half of their time in routine works. It however remains a mystery as to what happens to the remaining hours. Probably it is used (wasted) in unspecified works or devoted to such works which are not worth to be disclosed by them. The managers were ambiguous on this count.

As discussed in earlier pages, a manager should work at least six hours out of eight working hours. It is the maximum limit of capacity of an employee in normal course. Although not disclosed, it may be that the time robbers, specially 'leisure' and 'gossip' eat away the remaining half of the committed hours of the managers. They remain busy but not productive. This warrants a proper planning of allocation of tasks and time management. Although managers claim to work for minimum six hours (out of eight hours) a day, it is observed that most of their effective working hour is used (wasted) in routine and unproductive works. They remain busy all the time but total effectiveness is negligible. It seems they just work and never plan their working for getting a result. It is therefore suggested that manager should work for result and not for the sake of work.

Surprisingly, even after devoting so much time in performing routine works in office, on one hand and unaccounted working hours on the other, the managers (more than half) expressed to spend some time daily at home for discharging their normal work, especially paper work (Table 3.11). Such a trend leads to ambiguity. It may be time spent during office hours in the name of normal professional work is wasted in non-productive official works. Another probability may be that the managers have to fight with huge pile of paper works and they dispose them of peacefully at home. Another reason may be the officialdom or bossism which compels managers to bring files at home. They pretend to be extremely busy at office.

Such a routine is not a welcome sign. The managers should make a distinction between home and office, personal time and committed time. Every effort should be made to finish official work at office during working hours only. This demands a sincere planning of working hours by the managers. It reflects their apathy towards time. They plan their expenditure, they budget their income, they prepare daily or monthly financial balance sheet with all sincerity, but they don't have any time budget. This shows their lack of personal sense of time and value attached to every second.

Table 3.11
Time Spent at Home for Official Work

Responses	*Respondents (Percentage Distribution)*
Yes	60
No	40
Total	100

Holding Productive Meetings

Meetings, both of groups and between individuals are obviously essential. We cannot lead or manage without them. There are various sorts of meetings – briefing, advisory, council and committee, negotiating. They can be divided into categories roughly according to how decisions are taken. It is important to know what kind of meeting it is, but we should remember that a particular meeting may blend two or more of these basic types.

Meetings are essential, but they waste a large amount of management time. Meetings consume time in preparation and minute writing, as well as attendance. (Pearson: 1988) Some managers mortgage upto 50 per cent of their working time by taking part in regular meetings. Quite often monthly performance review meetings are spent largely discussing the results for the previous month, which are history. One can analyse and discuss actual results, but can't change history.

Everyday managers have meetings and appointments. Some of them are internal meetings, or just a brief meeting with the boss, or a co-worker. And other times, they have meetings with some one who is from outside organisation. These meetings may take place within manager's office, at their (other's) office, or some place in between, such as over breakfast, lunch or dinner at a restaurant. If manager is meeting with his boss, a colleague, or a co-worker, his meeting actually starts the moment he gets up from his desk to go to the meeting. Manager should be friendly and cordial and walk into the meetings on time with a smile on his face. A smile makes a lasting impression. (Mayer: 1995:83)

There is no excuse for meetings which don't start on time and which don't finish by the scheduled time, or for people who arrive late. This wastes time and is sloppy management, and should be stopped.

In group meetings, there are four specific types of questions that can be used to keep the group moving toward the intended objectives, to control it, and to draw out its best thinking. The overhead question is used to get the discussion started. It is thrown out to the participants in the hope that some of the smears talkative will catch the ball and run with it. It can also be a means of getting some one to summarise what has been accomplished up to a given point. A rhetorical question requires no answer. It is used to arouse interest, to focus attention or to impel the group to think more deeply. The returned question is which the manager leader may return and when he wishes to help the questioner find the answer himself rather than provide him with a neatly wrapped solution. When it is clear that the questioner is not capable of providing his own answer, the manager can relay it to the group as a whole. It is a redirected question.

The variety of questions is not of importance; the essential thing is that the manager-leader masters the art of asking the right question to the right person at the right time and in the right way. His real purpose should not be merely to secure the desired information but additionally to help others learn and to build a more cooperative relationship. (Cribbin: 1972: 176-7)

Meetings are not only an information regulatory mechanism, they act as instruments for discovering and sharing new ideas and finalise policies, mobilise resources, coordinate efforts, inform and guide people to achieve common goals. If you are keen to gain a reputation for holding decisive and effective meetings then not only will the people value this efficiency but the meetings will prove a fruitful mechanism for enhancing the productivity and performance, besides, ensuring smooth coordination at all levels. The business of the meeting, stated in the agenda, should be precise and concise. This form of publicity will emphasise to all that the meeting is about achieving defined goals. (Kharb: 2003: 98-100)

It is a common felling that the managers in public sector enterprises have some fascination of holding meetings. During the informal discussions it may be confessed that many of these meetings are purely gossiping session rather than having serious discussions. The issues may be trivial and routine but meetings are held and ended without any result or solution. Some times meetings are called urgently, discussions are held without any agenda and no minutes are prepared. Surprisingly, in many organisations managers face problem of spending the time and managers visit their peers or call them and hold meetings (gossip). Some managers read newspapers and magazines during office hours just to pass the time. Telephone calls many a times are made to discuss household chores and other matters which have no relation to the organisation.

Such a state of affairs in public sector enterprises deserves serious thought and proper redressal. Meetings are necessary hence be made productive. Agenda be prepared and circulated in advance for better appreciation of problems. Minutes of every meeting should be recorded and decisions taken be followed up and reviewed. The agenda of meetings held with top management is prepared and distributed. The decisions taken in such meetings are followed up. But in other meetings, the things are not sailed in proper way.

Table 3.12
Holding Meetings

(Percentage Distribution)

	Great Extent	*Some Extent*	*Not*	*Total*
Meetings are necessary and beneficial for smooth and efficient functioning	50	20	30	100
Meetings are productive	40	20	40	100
Agenda is prepared and distributed in advance	40	10	50	100
Minutes are recorded	30	20	50	100
Decisions taken are followed and reviewed	35	15	50	100

Personal Organisation

In fact, there is one area of our life over which we all have a great deal of power and that is time. We say time flies. The truth is that time proceeds at a fixed and regular rate. We like to save time by doing things in advance or taking shortcuts. We can't really hoard time. We speak of making up time; but what has passed is irreplaceable. Time goes, goes the saying, we may go on to something else, but time remains. We think of time as our 'mortal enemy'. We accuse it of being 'against us'. But it is on our side – the moment we organise it.

Getting started seems to be a very difficult task for many people. Procrastination is a long word for avoiding unpleasant tasks. Procrastinators are easy to spot; they are always open for interruptions and diversions. It is not surprising that they can never seem to meet a deadline because 'there is not enough time'. Visitors, meetings, phone calls, routine mail, idle chats, and a host of other things keep the procrastinator from doing what should be done.

Decision by committee is a time wasting habit developed by some managers. These individuals are reluctant to take the offensive in decision making. They would rather get a variety of opinions and then take a note. Although these are certainly occasions for participatory decision making, routine matters do not qualify.

Not following through is another habit that wastes time. Managers will find that it takes more time to correct an error than to make sure the work is done properly in the first place.

Breaking bad habits is not easy. But persistence and determination can produce dramatic results that will be well worth the effort. (Fulmer: 1988: 154-6) Planning the personal development presupposes the level of potentials among the managers. It is therefore necessary that managers should know their energy level.

Energy Level

The exact amount of energy that an employee possesses is usually a function of such variables as fatigue, efficiency of work, concentration, amount of work, listlessness, eagerness, and alertness. Unfortunately, these individual energy flow variables are extremely difficult to measure. Because of the difficulty in measuring these parameters, the HRD managers were asked simply to rate their energy level per hour on a scale from 1 to 10, 1 being the best rating. Most managers identified (Table 3.13) primary and secondary peaks, with the first peak at 9-12 am is 12 noon and the second peak at 4-6 p.m. However, there were some unusual responses.

HRD managers in many enterprises identify their secondary peaks as being higher than their primary peaks, a suggestion that these managers do more productive work in the afternoon rather than the morning. Another interesting result is in the magnitude of the energy level. Several managers indicate that they never achieve an energy level of 10. Generally, the corporations which have project-driven works and those that use well established historical standards for work appear to have the highest overall levels of energy. All managers feel a minimum level of energy at noon, the time for their lunch hour.

Probably, the most interesting result is that most HRD managers know their energy cycle. Many managers believe, for example, that they do their most effective writing in the morning and some their reading for the afternoon. It draws another conclusion that managers generally have low level of energy between 12 noon to 3 p.m. thus three hours out of eight hours with low energy level. This period consists of the rest break of half an hour. This makes clear that managers have break like situation spread over these three hours. However, it has been observed that many meetings are planned between 11 a.m. and 1 p.m. Thus period having low energy level is utilised in holding meetings.

If analysed variable-wise, it is interesting that efficiency of HRD Managers is at peak in morning hours (9 to 11 a.m.) and again started increasing after lunch break. Similar is the response in connection with concentrating at work. Listlessness and fatigue are found at peak between12 to 3 p.m. It is obvious that after putting on three hours in morning the Managers may need some rest. Once after lunch break this show reducing trend but again rise in the evening. It is very important to know one's own energy cycle.

Table 3.13
Energy level of HRD Managers

(Percentage Distribution)

Variables	*Peak*				*Hours*	*(time)*					
	9	10	11	12	1	2	3	4	5	6	Total
Efficiency of work	20	20	20	5	2	1	8	10	7	7	100
Concentration	16	20	15	10	3	2	5	7	10	12	100
More of work	20	20	20	9	3	2	4	8	8	6	100
Listlessness	9	3	2	10	20	22	15	8	6	5	100
Fatigue	3	3	2	8	25	23	10	5	9	12	100
Eagerness	15	15	20	8	5	3	7	12	10	5	100
Alertness	14	15	15	10	5	3	7	10	13	8	100
Energy level	**73**	**84**	**86**	**(-)24**	**(-)27**	**(-)34**	**6**	**34**	**33**	**21**	

** 9 a.m to 6 p.m.*

Energy Level per Week

Most employees do not perform at the same energy level each day of the week. Most officials feel that their peak performance days are Tuesday, Wednesday, Thursday and Friday. In most cases the energy level is lowest for Saturday and Monday. In many cases Saturday is rated as the highest level in regard to energy level because of getting the pre-determined job quota for the week completed by week end. Sunday was not considered for this analysis.

Table 3.14

Energy level for the week

(Percentage distribution)

Days	*High level*	*Medium level*	*Low level*	*Total*
Monday	25	45	20	100
Tuesday	57	32	05	100
Wednesday	60	35	05	100
Thursday	58	37	05	100
Friday	62	35	03	100
Saturday	40	47	13	100
Average (daily)	**50.33**	**38.50**	**6.00**	

The data depict that average high energy level per day is little more than 50 per cent. Major reason behind this may be the less work- load with the managers. This may be corroborated by the general observations that HRD wing in many enterprises is assigned the personnel maintenance functions only. The fresh recruitments are negligible in public sector companies and the matters related to personnel are dealt in a routine way. There is a need to plan and execute personnel development functions to enthuse the employees, sharpen their knowledge and upgrade skills.

Organisations are processing units which transform certain inputs from the environment into specified outputs desired by society. Every manager thus has the responsibility of organising subordinates into patterns of interactions that will facilitate accomplishment of unit goals. Human resource development implies that the input of human capital is more crucial determinant of organisational out-put than material capital. Also, it is infinitely amplifiable through releasing rather than control of energy. It has been increasingly felt that the total organisation should be viewed as a system and there should be efforts at long range improvement of the organisational culture. This alone would have a lasting effect on any major changes or innovations introduced in any organisation.

The organisational culture has two aspects – formal and informal. The formal aspects essentially involve the goals, technology, structure, policies and procedures, products and financial resources. On the other hand, the informal ones involve the perceptions, attitudes, feelings, values, informal interactions and group norms. In fact, it is the informal aspects which play a major role in the change that is envisaged in the total organisational climate. Under the changed scenario, HRD Manager has to act as a role model for his team consisting of all human resources working in the organisation. An HRD Manager first manages his development by managing his office hours. Then he should attempt to bring changes in attitudes and behaviour towards time in his immediate subordinates. Once his team practices managing the time, he should persuade his peers in other units to adopt time management strategy. In pursuance, an integrated time management plan for the whole organisation be formulated and implemented because time management of one manager in isolation can not be effective.

References

Bajaj, B.L. (1998), Time Management, Prashasnika, XXV (1), January-June, 33-40

Covey, Stephen, R. (1992), The Seven Habits of Highly Effective People, Simon & Schuster, London

Douglass, Merrill E. (1975), Creative Use of Time, The Personnel Administrator, October

Hibbard, Janet G. and Landrum, Robert K. (1978), How to Fight Time and Win, Personnel Journal

Mathur, K.M. (1993), Towards Effective Management (Pathways to Excellence), Gyan, New Delhi

Adair, John and Allen, Melanie (2003), Time Management and Personal Development, Viva Books Pvt. Ltd., New Delhi.

Pearson, Barrie (1988), Common-Sense Time Management for Personal Success, Mercury Books, Livingstone

Albrecht, Karl (1978), Successful Management by Objectives, Prentice Hall Press, New York

Kharb, Col. Karan (2003), Made to Lead, Wisdom Tree, New Delhi

Mayer, Jaffrey J. (1995), Time Management for Dummies, Pustak Mahal, New Delhi

Gribbin, James J. (1972), Effective managerial Leadership, American Management Association Inc., New York

Fulmer, Robert M. (1988), The New Management, Macmillan Pub. Co., New York

Oncken (Jr), William and Wass, Donald L. (1999), Management Time: Who's Got the Monkey? Harvard Business Review, November-December, 179-186

4

Managing Manager-leader

Modern manager is not simply interested in getting the things done; but leading the team and developing the individual alongwith his own development is his added responsibility. He is not neither an exclusive manager nor isolated leader but a composite manager-leader.

New Philosophy of Management

Managers at all levels are business leaders. The business is about producing quality products or services at a profit or in the most cost effective way. At the heart of that role lie the three overlapping core responsibilities of any leader: task, team and individual. A manager has certain tasks to perform. He facilitates team building and cohesive team- working. Manager is responsible for developing individual employee in his team for better accomplishment of organisational objectives. An individual should be developed in such a way that he assimilates his objectives into the objectives of the organisation. Thus manager of today has a new role as that of a manger-leader.

This three-circle model of leadership functions (Exhibit 8) integrates together what is customarily called leadership and

Managerial Responsibility

Source : Adair & Allen (2003), 4

management. This model implies an understanding of the environment in which manager is working, as well as the need to possess or develop the necessary qualities of personality character, and skills to provide the necessary leadership functions defining the objectives, planning, briefing, controlling, informing, supporting and reviewing. Thus there are often three elements in a manager's jobs – managing, leading and professional. (Exhibit 9)

The actual shape of the triangle in a manager's role circle will alter as his responsibilities developed or unfold. This particular concept or philosophy of leadership/managership places a very high premium on a manager being able to manage his time well.

According to Covey (1992), leadership is the first creation. Leadership is not management. Management is the second creation. Management is a bottom line focus: How can best

Exhibit 9
Elements of Manager's Job

accomplish certain things managers want to accomplish? In the words of both Peter Drucker and Warren Bennis, "Management is doing things right, leadership is doing right things". Management is efficiency in climbing the ladder of success, leadership determines whether the ladder is leaning against the right wall. Leadership is primarily a high powered, right brain activity. It's more of an art; it's based on a philosophy. Effective management is putting first things first. While leadership decides what first things are, it is management that puts them first, day by day, moment by moment. Management is discipline, carrying it out.

A manager-leader is sensitive to the fact that a principal means to return on investment is 'return on individuals'. The job of the manager is to be constantly concerned with performance, proficiency, productivity and profit. This in turn is the product of two factors: the competence of the work-force, multiplied by its motivation. In a sense, half of the manager-leader's task is to seek persistently to raise the competence level of his people. The second factor has to do with the manager's ability to motivate his people to become self starting achievers. Over and beyond this, the manager's role is that of a change agent, introducing innovations that will enhance the performance and promote the improvement of his work group, changes that would not occur in his absence. (Cribbin : 1972:4)

The Work of Leadership

There is nothing in modern society more vital than that of a manager. He is a planner, producer, marketeer and is the man who is expected to make things happen. He is the pivotal figure and the primary instrument in the technical task of the creation of wealth. Manager's dual personality as that of an employee and that of a citizen works in total environment. It is of vital importance that the manager must have a complete awareness and understanding of relationship with both its internal and external environments. These relationships are established and maintained in the spirit of mutuality, reciprocity and interaction. (Aggarwala: 1984:55-8) We have already discussed in earlier chapter the mutual interactions of an executive and organisation with varied environments.

The prime mover in the running of the management machinery is the executive. He is the very sap of life of an enterprise. It is through his dynamism and leadership that resources become productive. An executive as a leader analyses, clarifies, defines and lays down the goals or objectives for his group. He helps to create homogeneity within the work-group and the right atmosphere for the realization of these objectives. He shows the way and leads the group onward. The executive's role as a coordinator is to put the disorganized resources of men, machinery and money together into a useful enterprise.

He is the centre of activity for mobilizing the required resources, coordinating the activities within and outside the enterprise and encouraging the men to make greater efforts for achieving the common objectives.

Public sector enterprises in India today face many challenges, adaptive challenges, being one of them. Changes in societies, markets, customers, competition and technology around the globe are forcing these organisations to clarify their values, develop new strategies, and learn new ways of operating. Often the toughest task for leaders in effecting change is mobilizing people throughout the organisation to do adaptive work. Adaptive work is required when our deeply held beliefs are challenged, when the values that made us successful become less relevant, and when legitimate yet competing perspectives emerge. Adaptive challenges are seen everyday at every level of the work place. They are witnessed when marketing has difficulty in working with operations, when cross functional teams don't work well, or when senior executives complain of inability to execute effectively. (Heifetz & Laurie: 1997: 124-5)

Indeed, getting people to do adaptive work is the mark of leadership in the present competitive world. In order to make change happen, executives have to break a long standing behaviour pattern of their own: providing leadership in the form of solutions. Solutions to adaptive challenges reside not in the executive suite but in the collective intelligence of employees at all levels, who need to use one another as resources, often across boundaries, and learn their way to those solutions. Second, adaptive change is distressing for the people going through it. They need to take on new roles, new relationships, new values, new behaviours and new approaches to work. In the situation, rather than protecting people from outside threats, leaders should allow them to feel the pinch of reality in order to stimulate them to adapt. Instead of orienting people to their current roles, leaders must disorient them so that new relationships can develop. Instead of quelling conflict, leaders have to draw the issues out. Instead of maintaining norms, leaders have to challenge the way and help others distinguish immutable values from historical practices that must go.

Integrated Management

A manager-leader has responsibilities divided in three areas: organisation, team and own.

A manager has a responsibility to his organisation to help achieve business goals and realise the vision. A manager's key purpose or task is to achieve the organisation's objectives and continuously improve its performance.

One of the major challenges facing managers in the new millennium is dealing with the impact of flatter organisations where responsibility is devolved right across the work-force. Individual empowerment and team working are finally becoming a reality. Managers are no longer 'bosses' but leaders of focused teams who must earn the respect of their team members. Manager has a responsibility to his team to lead, support, develop and motivate them to realise the organisation's goals together with team goals and individual goals.

A manger is first a human being and then a manger. He has also a responsibility to himself to develop his potential to the full.

The manager enshrined with all these three roles, is an Integrated Manager. In the post-liberalised market dominated economy every manager (fiscal, material, human resource, public relations, sales, marketing etc.) has to be an Integrated Manager. An integrated manager is he who has the complete knowledge of working of his organisation. He should be a smart sales manager, a creditable materials manager, a dynamic human resource manager, an innovative public relations manager, a keen market manager, if need arises. A manager is not simply a manager, he should be a creative leader as well

Exhibit 10
Characteristics of Integrated Manager

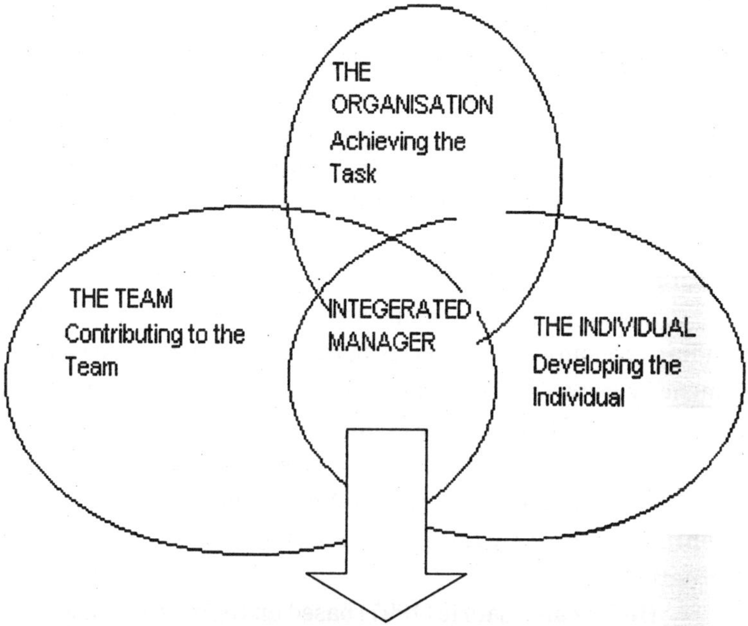

Showing concern for excellence
Setting and prioritising objectives
Monitoring and responding to actual against planned activities
Showing sensitivity to the needs of others
Relating to others
Obtaining the commitment of others
Presenting oneself positively to others
Showing self confidence and personal drive
Managing personal emotions and stress
Managing personal learning and development
Collecting and organising information
Identifying and applying concepts
Taking decisions

Source: Adapted from Adair & Allen (2003), 75

and also a high class professional. It is the multifaceted competence and high class managerial excellence which make a manager Integrated Manager. A manager should be a leader, developer, motivator, professional, worker, besides a manager. Success of a manager in this competitive era depends upon multi dimensional organisational personality and excellence. Adair and Allen have beautifully identified the characteristics of an integrated manager (Exhibit 10).

Principles of Leading

Leading is getting complex in the liberalised and globalised Indian economy. Public sector managers have to face a changed music everyday. In the present day scenario, managers have to adapt themselves and also make their subordinates adaptable. Every public sector enterprise has to be organised and managed on the lines of business organisations, otherwise they will left behind in the emerging competitive industrial economic situation.

Heifetz and Laurie (1997) based on their experiences with managers world over, offer six principles for leading adaptive work:

(a) *Get on the Balcony*

Manager-leaders have to be able to view patterns as if they were on a balcony. It does them no good to be swept up in the field of action. Leaders have to see a context for change or create one. They should give employees a strong sense of the history of the enterprise and what's good about its past, as well as an idea of the market forces at work today and the responsibility people must take in shaping the future. Leaders must be able to identify struggles over values and power, recognise patterns of work avoidance, and watch for the many other functional and dysfunctional reactions to change.

The dynamics of adaptive change are far too complex to keep track of, if leaders stay only on the field of play. In Indian public sector enterprises, managers even do not bother to be on the balcony, they keep always confined between the four walls. They see the field situation through the eyes of others.

(b) Identify the Adaptive Challenge

When businesses cannot learn quickly to adapt to new challenges, they are likely to face their own form of extinction. Thus identifying its adaptive challenge is crucial for any enterprise. For the strategy to succeed, the leaders need to understand themselves, their people, and the potential sources of conflict. Unfortunately, most of the public sector enterprises in our country have chosen the way of restraint rather than accepting the changes and adapt accordingly. Their rigidity is causing huge loss and thus disinvestments and a change in management, which in no case is a permanent remedy.

(c) Regulate Distress

Adaptive work generates distress. Before putting people to work on challenges for which there are no ready solutions, a leader must realize that people can learn only so much so fast. At the same time, they must feel the need to change as reality brings new challenges. They cannot learn new ways when they are overwhelmed, but eliminating stress altogether removes the impetus for doing adaptive work. Because a leader must strike a delicate balance between having people feel the need to change and having them feel overwhelmed by change, leadership is a razor's edge.

A leader must attend to three fundamental tasks in order to help maintain a productive level of tension. First, a leader must create a holding environment. Thus a leader must sequence and pace the work. Too often senior managers convey that every thing is important. They start new initiatives without stopping other activities or they start too many initiatives at the same time. They overwhelm and disorient the very people who need to take responsibility for the work. Second, a leader is responsible for direction, protection, orientation, managing conflict and shaping norms. Fulfilling these objectives is also important for a manager.

A leader protects people by managing the rate of change. A leader orients people to new roles and responsibilities by clarifying business realities and key values. A leader helps expose conflict, viewing it as the engine of creativity and learning. Further more, a leader helps the organisation maintain those norms that must endure and challenge those that need to change. Third, a leader must have presence and poise, regulating distress is perhaps a leader's most difficult job. The pressures to restore equilibrium are enormous. A leader must have the emotional capacity to tolerate uncertainty, frustration and pain. He needs to communicate confidence that he and they can tackle the tasks ahead.

(d) Maintain Disciplined Attention

Different people within the same organisation bring different experiences, assumptions, values, beliefs and habits to their work. This diversity is valuable because innovation and learning are the products of differences. No one learns any thing without being open to contrasting points of view. Yet managers at all levels are often unwilling to address their competing perspectives collectively. They frequently avoid paying attention to issues that disturb them. They restore equilibrium quickly, often with work avoidance maneuvers. A leader must get employees to confront tough trade offs in values, procedures, operating styles, and power.

Because work ảvoidance is rampant in organisations, a leader has to counteract distractions that prevent people from dealing with adaptive issues. Scapegoating, denial, focusing only on today's technical issues, or attacking individuals rather than the perspectives they represent are to be expected when an organisation undertakes adaptive work. Distractions have to be identified when they occur so that people will regain focus.

When sterile conflict takes the place of dialogue, a leader has to step in and put the team to work on reframing the issues. When people preoccupy themselves with blaming external forces higher management or a heavy work-load, a leader has to sharpen the team's sense of responsibility for carving out the time to press forward. When the team fragments and individuals resort to protecting their own turf, leaders have to demonstrate the need for collaboration. People have to discover the value of consulting with one another and using one another as resources in the problem solving process.

Of course, only the rare manager intends to avoid adaptive work. In general, people feel ambivalent about it. Although they want to make progress on hard problems or live up to their renewed and clarified values, people also want to avoid the associated distress. People need leadership to help them maintain their focus on the tough questions. Disciplined attention is the currency of leadership.

(e) Give the Work Back to People

All too often, people look up the chain of command, expecting senior management to meet market challenges, for which they themselves are responsible. Indeed, the greater and more persistent distresses that accompany adaptive work make such dependence worse. People tend to become passive and senior managers who pride themselves on being problem solvers take decisive action. That behaviour restores equilibrium in the short term but ultimately leads to complacency and habits of work avoidance that shield people from responsibility, pain and the need to change.

Getting people to assume greater responsibility is not easy. Letting people take the initiative in defining and solving problems means that management needs to learn to support rather than control. Workers, for their part, need to learn to take responsibility. A leader also must develop collective self confidence. Self confidence comes from success, experience and the organization's environment. The leader's most important role is to instill confidence in people.

(f) Protect Voices of Leadership from Below

Giving a voice to all people is the foundation of an organisation that is willing to experiment and learn. The voices from below are usually not as articulate as one would wish. Leaders must rely on others within the business to raise questions that may indicate an impending adaptive challenge. Thus, as a rule of thumb, when authority figures feel the reflexive urge to glare at or otherwise silence some one, they should resist.

In this backdrop it was thought pertinent to adjudge the leadership style having been practised by HRD Managers, covered under the study. They were offered a number of options as a single leadership style may not be solitary mechanism for leading. The responses are collected in Table 4.1. The analysis depicts that the public managers feel the lack of flexibility due to rules and regulations. The managers have very little scope. Employees today are more aware and organised. The trade unionism has created a complex situation before the managers. Even if they initiate some measures to innovate dynamisms in leadership, the peers resist. Sometimes things take a bad turn and untoward incidents take place.

Most of the managers working in public sector enterprises thus prefer just to follow the rules and directives of top management. They behave like passive managers, because the performance is assessed on the basis of time put in the company and not on innovations introduced and initiatives taken. The public sector enterprises function as top-down hierarchical organisations. The situation in private sector is some what little different.

In public sector enterprises in the guise of impracticality, managers refrain from taking initiatives. Managers in general lack enthusiasm and commitment and do not pay attention towards orienting employees to the organisational objectives, history, role in economy, functioning etc. Managers have failed to develop themselves as an organisation man. They are particularly concerned about their own job responsibilities where as they are supposed to be acquainted with external environments affecting organisation and internal environment linking to functioning of organisation and also to make the subordinates aware about these. The potential of employees is never assessed and performance is appraised subjectively. Managers keep themselves away from managing the conflicts. Even minor conflict areas are referred to the higher officials. They generally have a coterie of his 'yes men' who work as manager's eyes and ears. Such a leadership style being practised by managers need to be reformed and given a positive and active shape.

Table 4.1
Leadership style of Managers

(Percentage Distribution)

Variables	*Yes* *GE*	*SE*	*No*	*Not Practical*	*Total*
· Attempt to change context or create one	25	30	10	35	100
· Orienting employees about organisation's history and its good past	10	25	40	25	100
· Acquainting employees about the external environments	10	20	30	40	100

(Contd.)

(Contd. Table 4.1)

Variables	*Yes*		*No*	*Not*	*Total*
	GE	*SE*		*Practical*	
· Practising avoidance	40	20	30	10	100
· Becoming party	20	35	15	30	100
· Identifying new challenges	45	25	10	20	100
· Understanding people's potential	15	25	20	40	100
· Making people adaptive to changes	20	40	10	30	100
· Managing conflicts	50	30	10	10	100
· Shaping work-norms	55	25	5	15	100
· Making presence always felt	45	30	5	20	100
· Having emotional capacity to tolerate frustration	20	30	15	35	100
· Developing confidence	25	50	10	15	100
· Identifying distractions	25	30	10	35	100
· Developing sense of responsibility among employees	20	25	15	40	100
· Collaborating workers	10	15	25	50	100
· Making employees consultative	5	15	20	60	100
· Initiating people for problem solving	5	15	25	55	100
· Giving voice to people	5	10	60	25	100

GE - Great Extent

SE- Some Extent

As the classic corporation developed, it evolved with increasingly complex layers, divisions and departments. One of the consequences of the hierarchical work organisation was a work-force that paid more attention to the rules of the organisation and less to the goals of the company. That emphasis on conformity to rules and regulations as a surrogate for goals had four major effects: pseudo work, passivity, resentment and ambivalence, and greed. (Huseman & Goodman: 1999:39-40)

First among the effects on the work-force is a tendency toward doing pseudo work. In this case doing what looks good is more important than doing what is good. People are rewarded for 'putting in time'. Another effect of the top-down organisation on the worker is passivity. Passive employees follow the boss's lead. They wait for orders and only then execute. Workers like these don't make any mistakes because they don't take any chances. The third effect of the hierarchy in the organisation is resentment and ambivalence.

Taylor's scientific management prescribed that managers give subordinate employees concrete directions for what they were supposed to do and how they should do it. However employees resent being stripped of any decision making power. Concurrently the rules of the organisation make these same employees ambivalent about their work. So employees end up wallowing in the security of a regimented work organisation. The final effect of the hierarchical organisation is greed. Although the company may be falling down around them, losing profit margins, employees will complain about losing advantage of their way.

The respondent managers feel job security as the mainstay in public sector enterprises. Their responses to various questions analysed earlier reflect that Indian public sector organisations are basically hierarchical organisation. Rules and regulations prevail therein. They are organised purely on non-commercial business organisations, although many are productive units.

Trade unionism and its related impacts are rampant. Human resources are not fully motivated and committed. Hence many of the public enterprises are in deep water but employees are getting all sorts of advantages. Managers are therefore obliged to spend more time on routine works. These are basically boss-imposed and system-imposed times. Most of the enterprises are running in loss but the employees are getting their dues regularly. The non-productive recurring expenditure on maintaining human resources in many public sector units is leading to heavy loss, thus the public sector in the country is becoming white elephant with every passing day. There is a need to identify the problem areas, redress them and develop public sector enterprises on commercial line.

Leadership is Learning

Many efforts to transform organisations through mergers and acquisitions, restructuring, re-engineering, and strategy, work falter because managers fail to grasp the requirements of adaptive work. In short, the prevailing notion that leadership consists of having a vision and aligning people with that vision is bankrupt because it continues to treat adaptive situations as if they were technical: the authority figure is supposed to define where the company is going, and the people are supposed to follow. Leadership is reduced to a combination of ground knowing and salesmanship. Adaptive situations are hard to define and resolve precisely because they demand the work and responsibility of managers and people throughout the organisation. They are not amenable to solutions provided by leaders, adaptive solutions require members of the organisation to take responsibility for the problematic situations that face them.

Leadership has to take place every day. It cannot be the responsibility of the few, a rare event or a once-in-a lifetime opportunity. Leadership, as seen in this light, requires a learning strategy. A leader, with or without authority, has to engage people in confronting the challenge, adjusting their values, changing perspectives and learning new habits. The adaptive demands require leaders to take responsibility without waiting for revelation or request. One can lead with no more than a question in hand.

The Learning Cycle

The process of learning can be broken down into four stages and represented as a cycle. (Exhibit 11) It is a continuous process. None of these stages is effective on its own. A fully developed learner goes through each stage of the process in turn and arrives back at the first stage. Knowledge acquired from one experience adds to the next experience. Most people have a preference for particular stages because of their learning style preference. The learning styles – Activist, Reflector, Theorist and Pragmatist – fit with the learning cycle. (Adair & Allen: 2003:108)

Exhibit 11
Learning Cycle

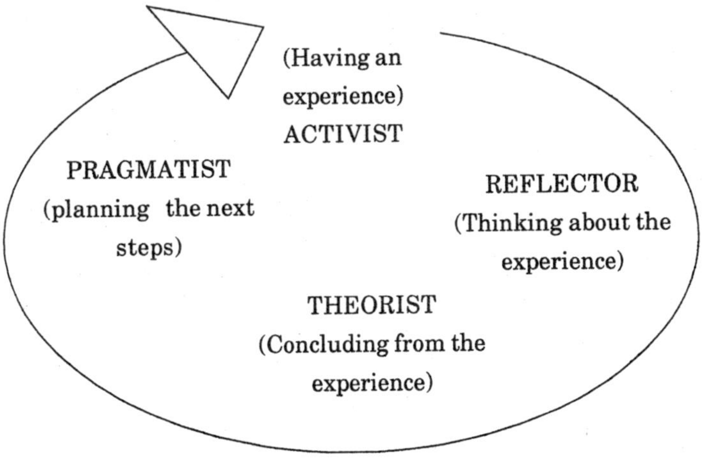

Source : Adair & Allen, 2003

If mangers are aware of their preferred styles and can understand where their weaker areas are, they can choose learning methods that will work for them or that will stretch them. They will also be able to understanding other people's learning preferences. No learning style is better than any other. Having a learning style preference simply means that this is the way you tend to learn.

Avoiding detailed, methodical work and paper work if at all possible, indicates an Activist tendency and respect and listen to other people's ideas indicates a Reflector tendency. Activists love new experiences. They tend to be enthusiastic about new ventures and experiences, flexible and ready to adapt. They will 'have a go' and jump into an experience, without always thinking of the consequences. They tend not to plan, but go from one activity to the next, thinking on their feet. They sometimes find it hard to sit still and they tend to get bored easily. They might start a project with great enthusiasm and then lose interest when they have to concentrate on the planning and the detail. They are always the first to have their say in meetings and have ideas easily in 'brainstorming' situations. They tend to be outgoing and gregarious, if a little self centered.

Reflectors like to have time to think about things from all angles. They like to collect as much information as possible about a subject before coming to conclusions. This often means that they take a long time coming to a conclusion. They like to put facts and information into perspective. In meetings they will be watching for the interactions of the people, as well as listening to ideas before they voice their own. They are thoughtful and wary of jumping into situations.

Theorists like to conceptualize their theories and their learning. They like to feel that whatever they do is founded on a sound rationale. They think in a step by step logical way and can go off on theoretical tangents, learning practicality behind. They like to analyse data and tide it up intellectually. They can be rigid and perfectionist and intolerant of emotional and subjective thinking. In meetings they tend to be quiet but attentive. If they have some thing to say, they will say it and stick to their guns through thick and thin. They can be irritated by flippancy and wary of unstructured situations.

Pragmatists like to be practical. They want to get on with the action rather than listen to theory. They tend to be intolerant of ideas and always get to the point. They are open to new challenges and like to solve problems and make decisions. In the push for practicality, they can be too hasty and go for 'quick fixes' rather than exploring other avenues. They like to work under their own steam and at their own pace and get great satisfaction from making ideas work. (Adair & Allen: 2003:109)

Table 4.2
Leadership Learning Style

(Percentage Distribution)

Indicators	*Yes*		*No*	*Not Practicable / Possible*	
	GE	*SE*			*Total*
· Identifying weaker areas	20	40	20	20	100
· Understanding other's learning preferences	10	30	30	30	100
· Avoiding methodical work	5	15	60	20	100
· Listen and Respect to other's ideas	10	30	20	40	100

(Contd.)

(Contd. Table 4.2)

Indicators	*Yes*		*No*	*Not Practicable/ Possible*	
	GE	*SE*			*Total*
· Love new experiences	20	25	10	45	100
· Flexible and ready to adapt	10	20	10	60	100
· Bored easily	20	30	50	-	100
· Lose interest in planning	5	10	5	80	100
· First to have their say	5	15	15	65	100
· Outgoing and gregarious	10	20	20	50	100
· Take time to think about	5	10	50	35	100
· Collect more data/ information	20	40	20	20	100
· Take long time to reach conclusion	5	10	40	45	100
· Conceptualise learning	5	5	10	80	100
· Rational and flexible	60	30	10	-	100
· Rigid and perfectionist	45	35	5	15	100
· Quiet and attentive	35	55	10	-	100
· Believe in action	50	45	5	-	100
· Ready to take decisions	20	30	5	45	100
· Have own working steam	5	10	10		75

GE- Great Extent

SE-Some Extent

As a part of the study, the managers were given a number of options reflecting characteristics of various learning styles. The respondents were requested to mark their learning style or their perceptions about them. The analysis in this regard highlights the enthusiasm and inquisitiveness among the managers. The only hurdle before them is in the form of rigidity in organisations. They cannot take any initiative of learning at their own. Every thing has to be got sanctioned from the top. Nothing is done beyond the wishes of the top management and the prevailing rules. Such a situation distracts managers from learning. That is the main reason that managers use (waste) most of their time in routine professional work. Many managers just pass the time.

Leadership Process

Setting direction is one of the primary roles of leadership. To be effective at this activity, the leader must be adept at perceiving not only environmental opportunities but also obstacles that stand in the way. Failure to do so will result in failed ventures and follies that discredit the leader. The leader must then be able to translate these opportunities into organisational goals and enlist organisational members in their achievement. In the enlistment process, the leader must be capable of realistic assessments of followers' needs and abilities and must ensure that targeted opportunities offer rewards meaningful enough to garner follower commitment and task efforts. (Conger & Kanungo: 1998:121-2).

To be effective, a leader must be capable of making realistic assessments of the environment. These assessments will in turn dictate the shape of initiatives and their timings as well as the resources the leader must seek out and where they will be deployed. Monitoring or assessing is a vital activity for the leader. It ensures that the leader is able to identify not only opportunities but also emerging problems and obstacles to the achievement of goals. The liaison role concerns itself with the manager's ability to establish relationships with individuals outside the manager's immediate work group. Although this network is crucial for implementing initiatives, it also serves as a rich source of information for the monitoring or assessment role. (Conger & Kanungo: 1998:123)

Furthermore, instrumental leadership concerns itself with three key activities: structuring, controlling and rewarding. In structuring, the leader activity builds management teams that possess the ability to execute and implement. The leader is also involved in creating structures that effectively convey throughout the company the types of behaviours required for the organisation to succeed. This activity revolves around detailed planning about roles and responsibilities, standards and goals. The second element, controlling, concerns the creation of systems to measure and assess both performance outcomes and behaviour. Finally, rewarding involves the administration of rewards and punishments so that performance and behaviour match the requirements of the change effort. (Nandler & Tushman: 1990:77)

When a leader fails to assess properly either constraints in the environment or the availability of resources, his or her strategies and actions may not achieve organisational objectives. For this reason, it is important that a leader be able to make realistic assessments of the environmental constraints and resources needed to bring about change within the organisation. This is where the knowledge, experience, and expertise of the leader become critical. A leader must also be sensitive to both the abilities and the emotional needs of followers – the most important resources for attaining organisational goals. (Kenny & Zacarro: 1983:683) After assessing the environment, a leader will formulate goals for achieving the organization's objectives. Charismatic leaders are often characterized by a sense of strategic vision. (Bass & Avolio: 1993) To be charismatic, leaders not only need to have visions and plans for achieving them but also must be able to articulate their visions and strategies for action in effective ways so as to influence their followers. (House: 1971)

In the final stage of the leadership process, effective leaders build in followers a sense of trust in their abilities and clearly demonstrate the tactics and behaviours required to achieve the organisation's goals. It is critical that followers develop a trust in the leader's vision. Generally, leaders are perceived as trustworthy when they advocate their position in a disinterested manner and demonstrate a concern for followers' needs rather than their own self interest. (Walster, Aronson & Abrahams: 1966) To be charismatic, leaders must make these qualities appear extraordinary. They must transform their concern for followers' needs into a total dedication and commitment to a common cause they share, and they must express this in a disinterested and selfless manner. They must engage in exemplary acts that are perceived by followers as involving great personal risk, cost and energy. (Friedland: 1964)

Leaders must appear to be knowledgeable and experts in their areas of influence. (Conger: 1989) They use their expertise in demonstrating the inadequacy of the traditional technology, rules and regulations of the status quo as a means of achieving the shared vision (Weber : 1947) and also in devising effective but unconventional strategies and plans of action. (Conger: 1985)

Promoting Cooperative Behaviour among Followers

Manager-leaders strive to build a strong collective identity among organisational members. This is principally because cooperative behaviour is essential for the mission of the leader. The demands of a lofty vision require highly effective team work and follower commitment that goes beyond the pursuit of individual gain. (Conger & Kanungo: 1998: 202) Cooperation also ensures heightened individual performance because organisational members are engaged to assist one another and to sacrifice their personal pursuits for the collective mission. (Kanter: 1967) The collective mission itself establishes norms for its members that put them under significant psychological and social forces that heighten their commitment to the mission. (Salancik: 1977)

The aim of such efforts is not only to heighten the sense of 'special ness' of the organisation but also to promote 'organisational citizenship behaviours'. These are discretionary behaviours that are beyond an individual's prescribed job responsibilities. (Conger & Kanungo: 1998:203) They include extra role behaviour designed to assist others in a 'good citizen' manner that 'in the aggregate promotes the efficient and effective functioning of the organisation'. (Organ: 1988:4) Extra role behaviours are critical because organisations are not able to anticipate through normal job descriptions. The complete picture of behaviours requires attaining their goals. (George & Brief: 1992)

Such extra role behaviours would appear to be a consequence of charismatic leadership whereby followers are highly motivated to perform beyond conventional performance standards. (Bass: 1985; Graham: 1988; Organ: 1988) As a result of this philosophy, a heavy emphasis is placed on team work as the primary selection criterion. In addition, information normally reserved for higher levels in the organisation is instead widely shared. (West & Garvin: 1993: 10-11)

At the same time, it is important to be realistic. Many charismatic leaders may simply lack the desire or discipline to become truly reflective. The strength of their own egos, their own passion, or the multiple and never ending demands on their time may prevent many of these leaders from undertaking active self examination and self monitoring.

Team Building

Organisations are made up of people working together to achieve some common end. Individuals working in isolation and in a separate way share no common goal. Team building can be applied within groups or at the inter-group level where activities are inter-dependent. The objective is to improve coordinated efforts of team members which will result in increasing the group's performance. The activities included in team building can typically include goal setting, development of inter-personal relations among team members, role analysis to clarify each member's role and responsibilities, and team process analysis. Basically, team building attempts to use high interaction among group members to increase trust and openness.

A crucial factor in group or team formation is the amount of time that is spent together. It takes time for a group personality to take place. Nature does not work quickly. Relationships are as tender as plants when young but as strong as oak when formed. Achieving a balance between the interests and self-expression of each individual on the one hand and of the group on the other is one of the most challenging tasks of leaders. The job of the manager is to bring a harmony and balance among the needs of the task, group as well as individual.

People's working abilities do not always match their qualifications. There are people in every team who have inclination towards particular activities. No one is totally useless. Only we fail to explore and tap the real talents of individuals. No one is evenly efficient in all fields. Managers should know their people to the core and dig out their efficiency and tap the real potential. If managers delegate work to individuals in accordance with their competence, they will certainly get good results. When managers delegate, they give a chance to the subordinate to prove his/her worth and at the same time to improve his/her calibre. Hesitation in delegating proves that managers do not have trust in their subordinates, nor do they have any interest in their (subordinates) professional improvement. Managers are thus working more and getting blamed too. (Kharb: 2003: 205-6)

It is interesting to observe that each unit is treated as a team. The works are assigned to each member of the unit (team) and a few operational authorities are delegated at the supervisory level. Decision making in general is more or less a centralized matter. Many managers find subordinates not capable to take decisions. Some finds them disinterested in accepting more authorities. The views of the employees are listened but most of their opinions are partisan. Managers are not having full freedom to form team of their own choice. They, however, make every effort to encourage team working with whosoever is put in their units.

Table 4.3
Encouraging Team Working

(Percentage Distribution)

Factors	*Yes*	*No*	*Not Necessary / Possible*	*Total*
Teams are formed	25	25	50	100
Members assigned work according to their potentials	15	35	50	100
Roles clearly defined	60	25	15	100
Encouraging team working	30	15	55	100
Establishing harmonious inter-personal relations	60	10	30	100
Understanding every member of team	70	10	20	100
Having personal relations with each member	70	10	20	100
Paying attention to every petty issues	65	5	30	100

(Contd.)

(Contd. Table 4.3)

Factors	*Yes*	*No*	*Not Necessary / Possible*	*Total*
Solving problems immediately	80	5	15	100
Inviting opinions from members	60	5	35	100
Associating employees in decision making	55	10	35	100
Respecting views of employees	65	20	15	100
Developing their skills	60	10	30	100
Delegating authority	50	10	40	100

Although managers claim to build teams and facilitate team working, in real sense there is less scope for team working. The whole organisation is classified on the basis of nature of work. Each department is further divided into working units. Every unit is assigned one or more works of homogenous nature. Managers probably treat these units as teams. The employees however are generally not oriented to team working. Each member of the unit (team) may be efficient but effectiveness of whole unit is found less the mark. The reason is that every member works in isolation. Each one concentrates on his job and has little concern with the working of others. This warrants a change in working style. Managers should develop the unit as team and every member is assigned clear roles and responsibilities. Role clarity and mutual trust are necessary for efficient team working.

Because managers are able to spend their time on their most important tasks, they are able to take control of their work and workday – it's no longer controlling them. Managers are able to see what's important and can set their own agenda. Managers are the one who is making things happen, and they are no longer just reacting to events as they occur. And after managers have taken control of the tasks and projects that need their attention today, they are in a position to begin planning for tomorrow and to look at these tasks and projects that will need their attention in the days and weeks ahead. (Mayer: 1995: 67)

There may be large responsibilities at home or in office for doing in a short span of time. To take up the entire project at one time may be too cumbersome. But if managers were to divide it into smaller segments and do it bit by bit, it will be done more easily and efficiently. The second part of this is to relinquish the idea of being selfish or jealous. Managers should help out others, whenever they need their help. As for their assignments, managers should make full use of their team. They should divide the assignment and share it as per expertise and experience of team.

Team work is the back bone of any organisation. As a collective effort, it involves everyone on the mission at hand. This integrates the team more cohesively and gives each member a sense of belonging and importance. Besides saving time, it also economizes on effort and enhances the quality of the out-put. This is how in a team a manager can go faster than time. Therefore, managers should utilise the time left behind for value addition, supervision and refinement. (Kharb: 2003:24)

Involving Employees

Employee involvement is a participative process to use the entire capacity of workers, designed to encourage employee commitment to organisational success. This process typically comes about by giving employees some combination of information, influence and/or incentives. (Cotton: 1993:3)

Employee involvement or participation is a relatively slippery concept. Given several forms and myriad definitions, many models of how employee involvement operates also have been developed.

Lowin (1968:69) defines participative decision making as a situation in which decisions as to activities are arrived at by the very persons who are to execute those decisions. In this model the effectiveness of involvement depends on the personality and attitudes of those involved; the extent, importance, and visibility of the issues addressed, and the quality of the participation process. Sashkin (1976) presents a model that focuses on the psychological target of the employee involvement. He first differentiates between four types of involvement (participation in goal setting, decision making, problem solving, and change) and argues that each can produce psychological and cognitive effects. These effects then lead to increased quality, acceptance and commitment, increased support for involvement, and an increased capacity of the organisation to adapt.

Locke and Schweiger (1979) present another model of the participation process. Their model differentiates between cognitive effects and motivational effects of involvement. These cognitive and motivational effects together produce higher productivity. In Schuler's model (1980) greater employee involvement serves to reduce role conflict and role ambiguity. The more involvement an employee has with his or her supervisor and fellow workers, the more chances there are for role clarification and role conflict reduction. Finally, the reduced role conflict and role ambiguity and the increased performance – reward expectancy should lead to greater satisfaction with the work and with the supervisor.

Leana (1987) differentiates between employee participation and delegation and presents data indicating that managers tend to use the importance of the decision and the characteristics of the subordinates in deciding whether to involve employees in participative decision making or to delegate. Tjosvold (1987) defines employee involvement as a subset of group problem solving. From this perspective, involvement can improve organisational effectiveness because several persons can increase the information and ideas considered and can develop higher quality solutions. For employee involvement to be successful, however, the employees must work together effectively. Conger and Kanungo (1988) address the concept of empowerment.

Effective performance in the directing of human activity and the exercise of control involve a psychological strain and pressure on the executive. The days of getting work done through the force of authority have gone. In the present atmosphere nothing succeeds like persuasion and appeal to the good sense of the subordinates. (Aggarwala: 1984:58)

The executive should have a basic knowledge of human behaviour and appreciation of its importance in directing human activities. The executive has no set of techniques for handling people. He has to use his own intelligence in understanding them and their point of view, and in dealing with them has to go by his own sense of what is fair and what is practical. The executive in modern management knows well the significance of good human relations in productivity and creativity. A small or trivial request or representation of an employee should be carefully listened to and considered.

It should be the constant endeavour of the executive to anticipate human relations problems. The executive should encourage participation of the people on whose performance depend the productivity, in the efforts to ensure better working conditions and living standards. Effective and timely communication serves to avoid any human relations problem from getting out of hand. To this end, the executive should keep himself in touch with the current trends is employee thinking.

Factors Affecting Involvement

There are many factors which influence involvement of employees. Some of the major factors are discussed hereunder.

Personality

Vroom (1959) was the first to attempt to study the effects of personality on reactions to employee participation. He found that individuals with weak desires for independent needs showed increased satisfaction when involved.

Participation process

Miller and Monge (1986) conducted a meta-analysis to examine what variables might moderate the relationship between employee participation and the outcomes of satisfaction and productivity. They focused on three general models: cognitive models, affective models and contingency models. According to them, cognitive models suggest that participation is effective because it enhances the flow and use of important information in organizations; affective models argue that participation is effective because it satisfies workers' needs and thereby increases satisfaction and morale; and contingency models propose that participation will affect satisfaction and productivity differently for different people and situations.

Wagner and Gooding (1987) performed additional analysis on their original meta-analysis to examine the effects of four situational variables – group size, degree of task interdependence, task complexity and use of performance standards – on employee participation.

Cotton et. al. (1988) employed the dimensions outlined by Dachler and Wilpert (1978) to distinguish between different forms of employee involvement. They divided their review into six groups: participation in work decisions, consultative participation, short-term participation, informal participation, employee ownership and representative participation. Their review found positive effects for participation in work decisions, informal participation, and employee ownership on permanence/ productivity. They found positive effects for informal participation and employee ownership on job satisfaction. Short-term participation and representative participation produced no effects for productivity or satisfaction, consultative participation had inclusive effects.

The managers express their willingness to make every attempt to involve their subordinates but a few of them find the level of employees not up to the mark and hence only a few experienced ones are associated with the development strategy. Managers admitl that decisions are predetermined either by the government in the form of policy or by the management board and the they are responsible only for their implementation in a proper perspective. This limits the scope of involving employees. The respondents on being asked as to whether the informations are shared with the employees, the managers divulged that informations pertaining to the working of the employees are unhesitatingly passed on to them in the form of directives but they are not burdened with informations unrelated to their respective working because such informations are totally irrelevant for them.

As regards incentives, the managers categorically find that all sorts of incentives already exist in their corporations. These incentives are granted under the provisions of the policy and management regulations. They however express their inability to grant any monetary incentives. All the monetary powers vest in the board. The managers in few cases are empowered to recommend the names for special incentives and final decisions are taken by the top management. Many managers however adopt non-monetary incentives to motivate their subordinates. They select best employee of the week or month. Their names are displayed at a board and kept at entrance. But such cases are not common. In many cases there are incidences of heart burning on this count.

As regards employee involvement in the organizations, it is somewhat satisfactory and encouraging but there is every scope for its increase. Managers should develop their subordinates and delegate generously so that they can save time for quality tasks.

Table 4.4
Involvement of Employees

(Percentage Distribution)

Indicators	*Yes*	*No*	*Not Required*	*Not Capable*	*Total*
Whether employees are involved	75	-	15	10	100
Monetary incentives exist	90	5	5	-	100
Non-monetary incentives provided	50	30	20	-	100
Informations are shared	50	20	20	10	100
Associated in problem solving	15	30	15	40	100
Employees are involved in identified conflicts	35	20	15	30	100
Employees are associated in role development	5	15	25	55	100
Employees are involved in individual development	10	20	20	50	100
Employees are ready to share responsibilities	15	35	-	50	100

Table 4.5

Extent of Employee Involvement

(Percentage Distribution)

Activities	*Great Extent*	*Some Extent*	*Not at all*	*No Scope*	*Total*
Employees associate themselves					
- in decision making	10	20	20	50	100
- in identifying conflicts/grievances	20	30	20	30	100
- in conflict/grievance redressal	20	30	20	30	100
-in solving operational problems	15	30	15	40	100
-in role development	5	15	25	55	100
-in individual development	10	20	20	50	100

Empowering Employees

The adopted strategy in the present perspective is the empowerment. There are many accepted ways to empower the employees.

Through Vision

The manager-leader formulates a vision that represents a clear purpose or mission for the organisation. For an organisational objective to be meaningful to members, it must represent a shared perspective. To achieve this shared perspective, the leader articulates the vision by anchoring it in a set of deeply held values of the members. The leader's articulation of the vision brings to the surface these deeply held values and makes the members realise that the vision is indeed a representation of their own values. The leader's articulation of the vision then is perceived not as foreign to the members but as a reflection of their own values they had never realised before. (Roddick: 1971:24) When organisational members perceive the vision as their own, they will feel internally driven to achieve the organisational objectives dictated by the vision. When the members perceive that the leader is the most articulate representative of their belief and values, they also develop trust and adoration for their leader.

Through Context Change

Another empowerment strategy a leader undertakes is to avoid or eliminate contextual conditions within the organisation that foster a sense of powerlessness among members. (Conger and Kanungo: 1998:197) The leaders must focus on removing the contextual factors from the organisation. They must institute organisational mechanisms and processes that make members feel empowered in the sense of having enough control over their environmental resources to make them effective within the organisation. Leaders can put in place mechanisms to promote an organisational culture that values free information sharing through participation and feedback systems, meaningful jobs through enrichment and goal setting programmes, and rewards for competent and initiative. (Conger & Kanungo: 1988)

Through Self Efficacy Information

The other empowerment strategy a leader pursues is to increase the sense of self efficacy among organisational members. Some informal practices on the part of leader can strengthen members' belief in their own capabilities to handle organisational tasks in innovative and effective ways. (Bandura: 1977) Leaders can structure organisational change programmes in such a way that initial objectives are sufficiently attainable and so that subordinates are able to execute them successfully. (Beer : 1980)

Words of encouragement, verbal feed back and other forms of social persuasion often are used by leaders to empower followers. (Conger: 1989) There is a limited scope in the hierarchy bound public sector enterprises in the country. Employees appreciate verbal encouragement to a limited extent. The managers therefore spend a little time to empowering their subordinates. The rigid rules and hierarchical limitations detract the often unwilling managers to adopt necessary measures for

Table 4.6
Empowerment of Employees

(Percentage Distribution)

Measures	*Great Extent*	*Some Extent*	*Not at all*	*No Scope*	*Total*
Formulation of clear objectives	30	40	10	20	100
Trust and Adoration	50	40	10	-	100
Eliminating sense of powerlessness	30	40	10	20	100
Information sharing	30	30	10	30	100
Increasing sense of self efficacy	20	30	5	45	100
Encouraging employees	45	50	5	-	100
Persuasion rather than authority	40	45	5	10	100

empowering the employees. Some managers are not easily accessible to employees. Many managers term the solving the problems of employees as empowerment. Unless and until managers manage their working hours and allocate time for every activity they will not be able to take care of the empowerment issues.

Right Man for Right Job

A key element of time management is recruiting a team of the calibre needed to achieve outstanding success. People who are over-qualified or over-talented for a position are likely to become bored with it quite quickly, and their performance is

Table 4.7
Placing Right Man on Right Job

(Percentage Distribution)

	Yes	*No*	*Inflexibility*	*No Need*	*Some Cases*	*No Response*	*Total*
Whether right man for right job practiced	40	-	60	-	-	-	100
Whether employees are over qualified	20	30	-	-	50	-	100
Employees are under qualified	10	60	-	-	30	-	100
Employees have appropriate caliber	60	40	-	-	-	-	100
Workaholic	70	10	-	-	-	20	100
Resultaholic	80	10	-	-	-	10	100
Both	85	-	-	-	-	15	100

likely to fall short of their ability. Unless managers have sufficient people of the appropriate calibre, it does not matter how effective their personal time management is, they may well end up working the hours expected of a workaholic and never see the situation improve. Managers should choose to be a resultaholic, not a workaholic. Resultaholics achieve more with less personal time and effort. Workaholics enjoy work, and often confuse it with results.

Developing People

Importance of developing personnel can well be highlighted from a Chinese saying: If you wish to plan for a year, sow seed; if you wish to plan for ten years, plant trees; if you wish to plan for a life time, develop men.(Bhatia: 1982) Employee development is the process whereby people learn the skills, knowledge, attitudes and behaviour needed in order to perform their job effectively. Along with scientific methods of recruitment, training is the principal means by which continuing high standards of performance is ensured in any organisation. Apart from equipping the personnel to do the regular routine work in the field, training should endeavour to create problem solving and innovation capacities. Correct training plays a critical role in promoting efficiency, changing attitudes of officials and in inculcating a better sense of service and probity in tasks. In a nutshell, training is an important tool for organisational growth. (Rao & Pareek: 1981)

More and more managers are learning that it is one thing to give orders but it is something else to have them carried out in a continuing, constructive, self correcting and quality assuring way. The importance of training in both individual and group performance has been underlined by the complex nature of modern society and liberalised and globalised economic system. If a skill or piece of knowledge is not already possessed it must be acquired. (Brown: 1965) Training may be thought of as a planned process whose organisational purpose is to provide learning experiences that will enhance employee – contribution to the goals of the organization. (Henemann & Schwabs: 1978)

There is no job in a modern society more vital than that of a manager. He is planner, producer and marketeer. He is the primary instrument in the technical task of the creation of wealth. Management development is the management of developing managerial ability in all functions, at all levels and in all departments of the organisation. It is the first and foremost responsibility of the highest level of management. (Kreiken: 1975) It encompasses the whole complex process by which managers as individuals, learn, grow and improve their abilities to perform professional management tasks. It involves learning on the job through experience. It is a planned effort to generate learning to help the organisation to monitor more effectively its change process. Individualised development plans, well meshed into organisational development effort are a pre-requisite to long term organisational effectiveness. (Goodstein: 1971)

The investment of time to train and develop people is another cornerstone of effective time management. (Pearson: 1988:58-70)Thus, the importance of training in developing employees is judiciously adopted. The objectives of training are to be derived from the objectives of the organisation. The first step in defining the objective is to identify the context in which the trainee works and in which training takes place. If people are trained to perform in a new way, but are not permitted to behave in the new manner in the work environment, the training is in- appropriate and wasteful. The pressures of the job unteach what is taught in the training class.

Apart from frustrating the training effort such a situation demotivates the trainees for all times to come. Therefore it is crucial to identify objectives by looking at the environment to which the trainee would be returning. Training objectives should be consistent with organisational objectives, climate and systems. The supervisory practices should support the trainee's newly acquired behaviour change and macro policy and procedures. Goals of the organisation would give validity and reinforce the application of the new learning on the job.

The efforts to help the individual bring about the changed behaviour after training, back on the job, are not enough. It is also equally important that necessary changes are brought about in the situation to which he returns. Often a trainee returns to his job completely frustrated, unhappy and doubtful of his ability to put his newly acquired knowledge and behaviour into practice under the prevailing situation of his organisation. So he magnifies the resistances, road-blocks and barriers, he faces or may face, thus drawing himself back to his original behaviour and becomes more disgruntled and frustrated.

Table 4.8

Arrangement for Developing People

(Percentage Distribution)

Indicators	*GE*	*SE*	*No Facility*	*No Need*	*Total*
Training opportunity available	20	60	10	10	100
Development Policy exits	10	30	60	-	100
SWOT analysis made	5	10	75	10	100
Orientation training given	10	40	40	10	100
Refresher training arranged	5	20	60	15	100
Experience sharing/Study tours arranged	2	10	80	8	100

GE - Great Extent SE-Some Extent

The HRD Managers feel that training and development in many enterprises is being treated callously and in an ad-hoc manner. There is no training policy as such. The HRD Managers are himself responsible for arranging upgradation of skills of employees. But they themselves are not fully exposed to new techniques. If there is any training opportunity the selection criterion for deputing personnel is quite subjective. Many managers express the need of having SWOT analysis to be made but they are apprehensive.

The managers should be facilitated to build and develop their capacity to deliver the more in less time.

People develop not only through better training but through the way organisation works. The job determines to what extent the person will be able to develop. The management should therefore, develop a working environment within the organisation, which will encourage personal growth and development as well as creative thinking. (Asthana: 1964) Many aspects of life have a significant influence upon behaviour. In fact basic values are so well ingrained that they have become very difficult to change. They influence the amount of education the employee seeks, how hard he works on the job, and the way in which he cooperates with fellow workers and managers. The basic relationship here is that of culture, of the job affection – the job performance. The job itself is the pre-eminent means for eliciting motivated behaviour. Increasing job challenge is itself the most powerful behaviour change technique at the manager's disposal. (Smith: 1977)

Getting Best out of Subordinates

To improve the efficiency within organisations it is necessary to make the best use of the available human resource. The starting point is to evolve techniques to select the right man for the right job. Secondly, a new employee faces a number of problems of adjustment. He has to adapt himself to organisational conditions. Thirdly, the workers have to be developed to scent the purpose of the organisation. Fourthly, for retaining the employees, better promotional avenues are a must. In absence of any opportunities for promotion, they may just work in the organisation but they will not put in their best. (Desai: 1969)

At the time of selecting an individual for a job in the organisation, the aim should be to retain him till he retires. Therefore, a clear vision about his future progress is very necessary. On the other hand, the management expectations should also be made clear to the employee at the very out set. Secondly, the selection of the exceptionally qualified person should not be made simply because he is available. Generally, such persons do not stay with the organisation for a longer time. They will not have the sense of belongingness with the organisation simply because they take the job temporarily and do not find it challenging or stimulating. The job becomes a problem not only for the extra qualified person but also for under qualified person. Therefore adequately qualified persons should only be appointed. (Singh: 1992.25)

What becomes more important than the leader's own ability is the question of how effectively he manages to get his men to make use of their abilities. Since this can be accomplished only through highly personal contacts, it depends on how good is the leader's hold on his immediate subordinates and, in turn, how skillful is he in leading the men under his direct control. (WED: 1981:42)

There are two dimensions of getting most out of the subordinates. First dimension is the preparedness of employees to deliver the best according to their capacity and capability. This requires high level of motivation amongst employees. The organisational environment should be created in such a way that a culture is developed which helps motivate the employees. Motivation should be a mix of monetary as well as non- monetary incentives. Second way is the capability of supervisor to get most out of his subordinates. This is an art. To develop such an environment the manager himself has to be committed to work devoted to the cause of the organisation and also towards the matters related to his subordinates. He should have faith on his subordinates and the subordinates should also have faith on his manager. For creating a sense of faith, manager should establish personal relations with each of his subordinates.

Managers should try to help subordinates in personal matters also. In organisation, manager should be a good listener. Even a small advice of subordinates should be given due importance and consideration. Outright rejection of views of subordinates demotivates them and they develop a habit of unconcern and listlessness. Simultaneously, managers should be able to sort out the problems of employees. He should be competent and knowledgeable. Manager should command the respect of his subordinates. Manager should lead his subordinates, manage the team of his subordinates and their work assignments, guide them in circumstances, help them in needs and develop them unjealously. This all can be achieved only when the manager is himself knowledgeable, competent and prepared.

The managers categorically accept to make efforts to get the most out of their subordinates. The completion of works assigned to employees is, surprisingly, treated by managers as the best out of employees. They claim the performance of their subordinates to be satisfactory but the managers express the non-availability of any measure to assess the potential. Unless and until the potentials are known the best can not be got. Managers have personal relations with their subordinates, hence exists a cordial working environment in the organisation. The views of subordinates are heard and considered. This is an illuminating trend. Managers claim to attend even petty grievances of their subordinates. This may reduce conflict and resentment among employees.

Table 4.9
Getting Most out of Subordinates

(Percentage Distribution)

Indicators	*Yes*	*No*	*Complete assigned work*	*No mechanism to assess their potential*	*Not equipped*	*Total*
Subordinates deliver their best	30	10	40	20	-	100
Potential Exists	25	15	-	60	-	100
Performance Satisfactory	60	5	35	-	-	100
Do you have personal relations with subordinates	80	20	-	-	-	100
Their views heard and considered	50	30	-	-	20	100
Petty grievances attended immediately	60	40	-	-	-	100

This all show the attempts having been made by managers to get the best out of their subordinates. If the managers succeed in getting the best of employees, they may save a lot of time out of their committed hours. Time thus saved can be used some where else effectively.

Thus, it is seen that manager-leader can save a lot of time out of their committed hours if they are efficient in their working. For the purpose, managers should assign jobs keeping in view the potential, suitability and attitude of the subordinates. The employees should be exposed to training and development efforts, as investment in training is one important factor in efficient time management. The subordinates be involved in decision making and team working be encouraged to motivate them to put best of their capacities. For building capacities and developing capabilities amongst employees, managers should play a lead role. They themselves should be competent and knowledgeable. The managers should practice delegation. All these measures can help managers save a lot of time out of their committed hours. This time can be used effectively in some other productive work.

References

Aggarwala, Dharma Vira (1984), Management, Deep & Deep, New Delhi

Heifetz, Ronald A. and Laurie, Donald L. (1997), The Work of Leadership, Harvard Business Review, January-February, 124-134

Conger, Jay A. and Kanungo, Rabindra N. (1998), Charismatic Leadership in Organisations, Sage, London

Nandler, D.A. and Tushman, M.L. (1990), Beyond the Charismatic Leader: Leadership and Organisational Change, California Management Review, 32, 77-97

Kenny, P.A. and Zacarro, S.J. (1983), An Estimate of variance due to traits in leadership, Journal of Applied Psychology, 68, 678-85

Bass, B.M. and Avolio, B.(1993), Transformational Leadership: A Response to Critiques, in M.M. Chemers and R. Ayman (eds) Leadership Theory and Research: Perspectives and Directions, Academic Press, New Delhi, 49-80

House, R.J. (1971), A path-goal theory of leader effectiveness, Administrative Science Quarterly, 16, 321-39

Adair, John and Allen, Melanie (2003), Time Management and Personal Development, Viva Books Pvt. Ltd., New Delhi

Cribbin, James J. (1972), Effective Managerial Leadership, American Management Association, Inc. New York

World Executive's Digest (1981), Management Japanese Style,Makali, Manila

Walster, E., Aronson, D. and Abrahams, D. (1966), On Increasing the Persuasiveness of a Low Prestige Communicator, Journal of Experimental Social Psychology, 2, 325-42

Friedland, W.H. (1964), For a Sociological Concept of Charisma, Social Forces, 43, 18-26

Conger, J.A. (1989), The Charismatic Leader: Behind the Mystique of Exceptional Leadership, Jossey Bass, Francisco

Weber, M. (1947), The theory of social and economic organisation, Free Press, New York

Conger, J.A. (1985), Charismatic Leadership in Business: An exploration study, unpublished doctoral dissertation, School of Business Administration, Harvard University

Roddick, A. (1991), Body and Soul, Crown, New York

Conger, J.A. and Kanungo, R.A. (1988), The Empowerment Process: Integrating Theory and Practice, Academy of Management Reviews, 13, 471-82

Bandura, A. (1977), Self-efficacy: Toward a Unifying Theory of Behavioral Change, Psychological Review, 84(2), 191-225

Beer, M. (1980), Organisational Change and Development: A Systems View, Goodyear, Santa Monica

Conger, J.A. (1989), Leadership: The art of empowering others, Academy of Management Executive, 3(1), 17-24

Kanter, R.M. (1967), Commitment and social organisation: A Study of Commitment Mechanisms is utopian communities, American Sociological Review, 33(4), 499-517

Salancik, G.R. (1977), Commitment and the control of organizational behaviour and belief, in B.M. Staw and G.R. Salancik (eds), New Directions in Organizational Behavior, St. Clair, Chicago

Kharb, Col. Karan (2003), Made to Lead, Wisdom Tree, New Delhi

Mayer, Jeffrey J. (1995), Time Management for Dummies, Pustak Mahal, New Delhi

Bass, B.M. (1985), Leadership and performance beyond expectations, Free Press, New York

Graham, J.W.(1988), Transformational Leadership: Fostering follower autonomy, not automatic followership, in J.G. Hunt, B.R. Baliga, H.P. Dachler and C.A. Schriesheim (eds), Emerging Leadership Vistas, D.C. Heath, Lexington, M.A., 79

Organ, D.W. (1988), Organizational Citizenship Behavior: The Good Soldier Syndrome, Lexington Books, Lexington M.A.

George,J.M. and Brief, A.P. (1992), Feeling good-doing good:A conceptual analysis of the mood at work-organizational spontaneity relationship, Psychological Bulletin, 112, 310-29

West J. and Garvin, D.A. (1993), Serengeti: Entrepreneurship with Corning Inc, Harvard Business School, Boston

Huseman, Richard C. and Goodman, John P. (1999), Leading with Knowledge (The Nature of Competition in the 21st Century), Sage, London

Cotton, John L. (1993), Employee Involvement (Methods for Improving Performance and Work Attitudes), Sage, London

Covey, Stephen R. (1992), The Seven Habits of Highly Effective People, Simon & Schuster, London

Pearson, Barrie (1988), Common Sense Time Management for Personal Success, Mercury Books, Livingstone

Desai, K.G., (1969), Human Problems in Indian Industries, Sridhar Publication, Bombay

Singh, U.B. (1992), Human Resource Development, Rawat Publication, New Delhi

Bhatia, S.K. (1982), Trends in Training and Development, Lok Udyog, XVI (1), 37-41

Rao, T.V. and Pareek, U. (1981), Designing and Managing Human Resource Systems, Oxford and IBH, New Delhi

Brown, D.S. (1965), The Important New Role of Training, Indian Journal of Public Administration, XI(1), 194-198

Henemann, H.G. (III) and Schwab, D.P. (1978), Perspective on Personnel/Human Resource Management, Richard D. Irwin, Inc, Illinois

Kreiken, J. (1975), Top Management's Role in Management Development, in B. Taylor and G.L. Lippit (eds), Management Development and Training Hand Book, McGraw Hill, New York

Goodstein, L.D. (1971), Management Development and Organizational Development, Business Quarterly, Winter, 6-13

Asthan, P.W. (1964), Developing Reliable Human Resources, Personnel Journal, 43(4), 185-188

Smith, H. P. and Bronwer, P.J. (1977), Performance Appraisal and Human Development (A Practical Guide to Effective Managing), Addison-Wesley Pub. Co.,

5

Managing Decisions

Decisions are part of human life. In every sphere of life, one has to take decisions. Time is an important factor in decision making. Time can influence decisions but not the vice versa. Decisions in turn affect life. Thus time, decisions and life are mutually inter-affected.

Time in Decision Making

A major part of the executive's time is taken up by decision making. In every phase of his work, the executive has to be the decision maker. While playing this role he must have a clear conception of the problem, analyse it well and have alternative courses of action in view, before arriving at one he deems best in the circumstances and starting the process of implementation. Decision making requires broad vision, knowledge, experience and intelligence which the executive has to cultivate through practice. Time is of paramount importance in business decisions. (Aggarwala : 1984: 59-60)

Managerial performance is judged on the basis of how many resources are used to accomplish an organisation's objectives. Decision making is the conscious deliberation about alternative ways to use resources. Because resources are limited, the capacity of managers to exploit opportunities is limited; everything cannot be tried randomly or haphazardly. Decisions are made to discriminate rationally among available alternatives.

Managers at all levels of organisation and in all functions within organisation deliberate among alternative actions. Decision making runs vertically from top management to first line supervision, and cuts horizontally across areas of specialization such as human resource development, industrial relations, sales, finance and production. Decision making is dynamically involved as a linking process, for it tries one function to another. The decisions of one manager or organisational unit are never made in isolation. Their implications and outcomes are related to other decisions throughout the organisational system. Decision making is an indispensable part of a system's approach to management. It is basic to every function of management; the job of management cannot be understood unless the nature of decision making is appreciated. (Haimann, Scott and Connor: 1978: 501-2)

Whatever a manager does he does through making decisions. Thus management is always a decision making process. Most tactical decisions are both more complicated and more important. But the important decisions, the decisions that really matter, are strategic. They involve either finding out what the situation is, or changing it, either finding out what the resources are or what they should be. These are the specifically managerial decisions. Strategic decisions, whatever their magnitude, complexity or importance, should never be taken through problem solving.

Decision making has five distinct phases: defining the problem, analysing the problem, developing alternate solutions, deciding upon the best solution, converting the decision into effective action. (Drucker: 1954: 331-3) Making decisions can either be time–wasting or it can be the manager's best means for solving the problem of time utilisation. Time should be spent on defining the problem. Time is well spent on analysing the problem and developing alternate solutions. Time is necessary to make the solution effective. But much less time should be spent on finding the right solution. And any time spent on selling a solution after it has been reached is sheer waste and evidence of poor time utilisation in the earlier phases.

Effective decision making is straight forward, but the implementation may be difficult, risky or unpleasant. It is often the implementation involved which causes people to choose the easy option or to put off making a decision. Effective decision makers are alert to which are the key decisions that should be made and which major opportunities should be explored because they keep themselves informed. (Pearson: 1988)

Two organisational variables affect decision making – the kind of job performed and the manager's level in the organisational structure. (Drucker: 1974:470) As a rule, higher the managers in the organisations, greater are their authority and discretion. As the managerial hierarchy is ascended, broad, complex problems that defy routine or detailed solutions are encountered. Decision criteria are vague, and solutions to decision problems are ordinarily given in terms of policy guidelines. Under these circumstances, the boundaries of rationality are fewer and looser for upper management. Consequently, there is opportunity for creativity and innovation in the decision making process. According to Drucker(1974), a decision is a judgment. It is a choice between alternatives. It is rarely a choice between right and wrong. It is at best a choice between 'almost right' and 'probably wrong' – but much more often a choice between two courses of action, neither of which is probably more nearly right than the other.

It is through rational decisions that we take charge of our lives. It is the cumulative effect of millions of decisions we continually take in our daily activities that determines the shape of our lives. Some times, even decisions having long-term effects on our lives are greatly influenced by emotions and enthusiasm which may evaporate over time. The new realities can create a shift in one's inclination and decision making mechanism. In fact, most of the problems in life occur because we fail to take the right decision at the first opportunity. Life is just another name of action. Action is the product of decision. Without decision it is impossible to act. An opportunity not treated well becomes a problem. We must therefore respect opportunities. Decision making presupposes courage to accept a challenge and risk. (Kharb: 2003)

Operational Management by Objectives

The job of the operational manager (in our case HRD Manager) differs from that of the top manager only in degree. The operational manager must do virtually everything the top manager does for his own unit, but the relative emphasis differs. Whereas the top manager is highly concerned with the basic direction of the entire organisation, the unit manager is concerned with the basic direction of his own group within the framework of the larger organisation. Both must concern themselves with the match between their respective organisations and their environments, both must set objectives, both must plan for their accomplishment, and both must evaluate results and give day-to-day guidance to their employees.

There are three categories of works which the manager can influence and recognise that the first and biggest category is largely self guiding. These categories are illustrated in Exhibit 12.

It is clear from the discussions in preceding pages that managers have no specific objectives. They work for accomplishing the major objectives set for the organisation. For want of clarity and specificity in the objectives, managers lack role clarity to a great extent. They are even not able to set

Exhibit 12
Categories of Work Activity

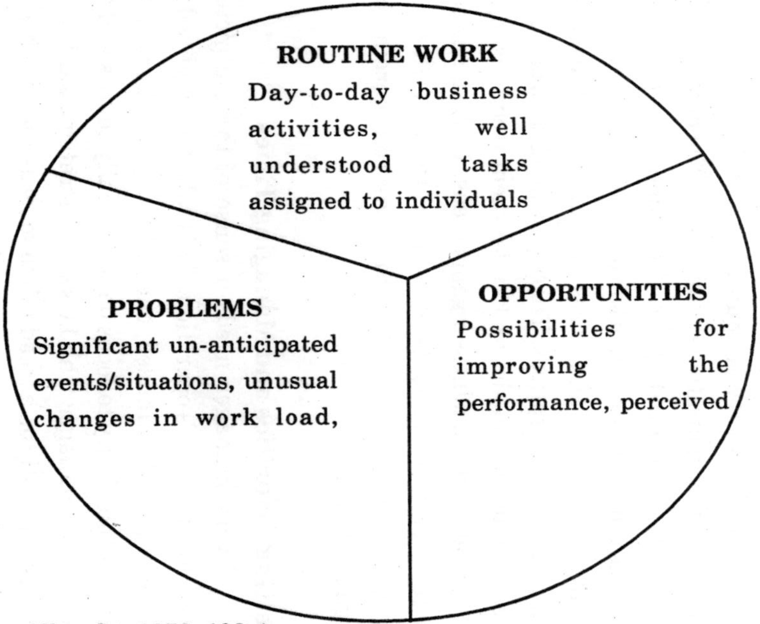

Source: Albrecht, 1978, 132-4

their goals and plan their accomplishment. It becomes thus imperative to assess the pattern of allocating time by managers for different activities. Although managers confess not to make any time budget, they give more emphasis on day-to-day routine works. It is in tune with the characteristics of working of the public sector enterprises.

The flexibility in public sector is very little in the hierarchical organisational framework. The managers therefore have little to contribute in the name of improvement and innovation. Fewer opportunities, missing challenges and rampant problems and crises are the main characteristics of public sector enterprises. There is a need to break away from the bureaucratic model and make them free to compete with the private sector business organisations. In the name of welfare, public sector should not be allowed to grow as a white elephant. It is high time to develop them as commercial business organisations.

Setting Priorities and Managing Times

Every manager needs a sense of the big picture with respect to the unit's operation. This calls for a highly developed sense of priority. Indeed, one of the most critical managerial skills is the ability to focus on what really counts and to find it first. The manager who lacks this strategic skill of focusing energy is usually on a treadmill to some extent. Such a manager is usually oversupplied with matters which demand his attention and undersupplied with time to think about the organisation and where it is going.

The manager and the organisation operate perpetually in the crunch mode. Fire fighting and crises operation become the organisational norm. Such a manager and his employees are mis-oriented. They lack a clear sense of direction. They focus on doing, not on going. The objectives- oriented manager

Table 5.1
Allocating Time on Different Activities

(Percentage Distribution)

Activity	*Extent of Emphasis*			*Total*
	Great Extent	*Some Extent*	*Not at all*	
Day-to-day routine activities	60	30	10	100
Assigned tasks	70	30	-	100
Working level problems	80	20	-	100
Jobs leading to improvement	60	30	10	100
Adaptive tasks	45	30	25	100
Crises	80	20	-	100
Change in work load	60	25	15	100
Change in policy	80	15	5	100
Change in environment	60	30	10	100
Change in management	70	30	-	100

manages a result department. The manager and the employees produce results. They operate with a strategic sense of pay off. (Albrecht: 1978: 135) The HRD Managers in public sector enterprises seldom show much concern to achieving the overall organisational objectives rather they are much particular about their job responsibilities.

The skill of time management enables the manager to develop and maintain this strategic sense. Time management requires that the managers maintain an organised written list, and use the list as a guide for doing first things first. Alan Lakein (1973) suggests that a manager ranks the things to do in three categories:

1. 'Must do' items
2. 'Should do' items
3. 'Might do' items

Lakein further suggests that the managers grant first priority status to only a few items, with a larger number assigned to the second category, and a still larger number assigned to third priority. A manager skilled in time management will frequently review the list of things to do and will find ways to combine items or to accomplish two or more of them at the same time. Such a manager will also question every single item as it arises, to decide whether it really needs doing and whether it can be delegated to some one else. This amounts to an assertive attitude towards the demands of the work environment.

The manager continually makes choices about how to spend valuable time and about how to get the highest pay off for that time. The effective time manager will scrutinize all miscellaneous activities and time wasters and eliminate them if they do not meet some reasonable pay off criteria. By attacking the things to be done in priority order, the manager ensures that, when time or energy runs out, any neglected items will cause only a minimum loss of opportunity or minimum inconvenience.

Having learned the time management discipline, the manager can train the employees of the organisation to manage their time effectively as well. In giving assignments, the manager can grant them an appropriate degree of freedom in scheduling the work, so they can arrange their daily activities largely as they see fit. In a broader sense, the manager keeps the employee's attention focused on key result areas, which offer maximum pay off potential. The objective-oriented manager recognises that there are usually more things to be done than time and energy permit and that not all the possibilities offer equal pay off. In setting the major objectives for the unit, the manager identifies those which offer the highest available pay off and concentrates resources on their achievement. (Albrecht: 1978: 137)

The managers unanimously feel that their priorities generally have no standing (Table 5.2). They can plan and prioritise jobs related to operational level only. They plan some thing but have to do some thing else as the situation demands. Their whole planning and priorities are dismantled almost every day. The managers find that there is no flexible opportunity for classifying the activities, as procedures are pre-defined. Every thing is pre-determined and managers have to get the things done accordingly.

They do sometimes informally classify activities on the basis of priority and availability of time and urgency involved but the subordinates undertake activities as per their requirement. The managers have to basically perform managerial functions and there is little scope for classification. Even in need of hour they do such exercise. Everything assigned to them is important and they have to perform them. In time of urgency such classifications are made just to manage the

Table 5.2
Classifying Activities

Classifications of Activities	*Most Focus*	*Normal Focus*	*No Focus*	*No Scope*
'Must do' activities	√			
'Should do' activities		√		
'Might do' activities			√	
Important activities		√		
Urgent activities	√			
Routine	√			

urgency. The managers therefore need a proper orientation towards effective planning and their time.

Decision Making by Objectives

The manager can also use the objectives orientation in dealing with decision issues which arise. The objectives orientation helps the manager to balance the need for positive action with the need to make sound decisions which stand the test of time. Decision making 'speed' forms an important part of every manager's general approach to problem solving. As figure illustrates (Exhibit 13), individual managers range from overcautious to overhasty in choosing a cause of action. This decision making style tends to be fairly consistent for any individual.

Those who ponder interminably over even the simplest decisions, who put off decisions, who can call for more and more fact finding and analyses, and who foster never ending debates seem paralyzed. They generally fear the accountability that comes with deciding. They end up in a state of 'paralysis by analyses'. Conversely, those who make snap judgments, who offer quick opinions, who always seem to have the solution, and who generally shoot from the hip; usually lend up going 'extinct by instinct'. These people enjoy the sense of quick action and try to convey an image of being mentally sharp and sure of them.

Both of these extremes are equally disastrous. The objectives-oriented manager can use the principle of creative procrastinations in approaching major decision issues. This attitude leads to a strategic approach to major decisions. The manager refuses to be stampeded by pressures for quick action, but also accepts the inevitable risk and uncertainty associated with every decision. Such a manager uses time constructively to anticipate major decisions and to study them in depth so as to clarify the various options. (Albrecht: 1978: 139-40)

Exhibit 13

Managers in Decision Making Style

OVERCAUTIOUS	MATURE	OVERHASTY
O ←	O	→ O

PARALYSIS BY ANALYSIS	GOING EXTINCT BY INSTINCT
Procrastinating	Making snap judgments
Evading decisions	Ignoring important facts
Studying issues exhaustively	Under estimating complexity
Shifting responsibility	Refusing to confer with other

Source: Adapted from Albrecht, 1978, 140

As regards pattern of decision making by HRD Managers in public sector enterprises, managers are found quite cautious. Although most of them express their willingness to take responsibility, in practice they transfer the responsibilities. In absence of role clarity and job responsibility, it is easy to shift responsibility, especially on subordinates. They all claim to take quick decisions but after studying all the dimensions exhaustively. They don't want to take any risk. The snap decisions or no decisions are preferred.

Taking a decision makes a manager pro-active, but many of them want to be passive decision makers. They prefer the decisions to be taken by the top management. Managers however do take decisions of petty nature which have no worth feeling impact. Probably, rules and regulations are the main hindering factors. In case of no decisions or delayed decisions, time is unnecessarily wasted. The delayed decisions have bearing on productivity of enterprises.

Table 5.3

Decision Making Style of Managers

(Percentage Distribution)

Indicators	*Emphasis*				
	Great Extent	*Some Extent*	*Not at all*	*No Scope*	*Total*
Procrastination	60	20	20	-	100
Evading decisions	20	30	40	10	100
Studying exhaustively	70	20	10	-	100
Taking responsibility	25	30	40	5	100
Making group decisions	65	25	10	-	100
Confer with others	35	20	25	20	100

Exhibit 14
DECISION MAKING MODEL

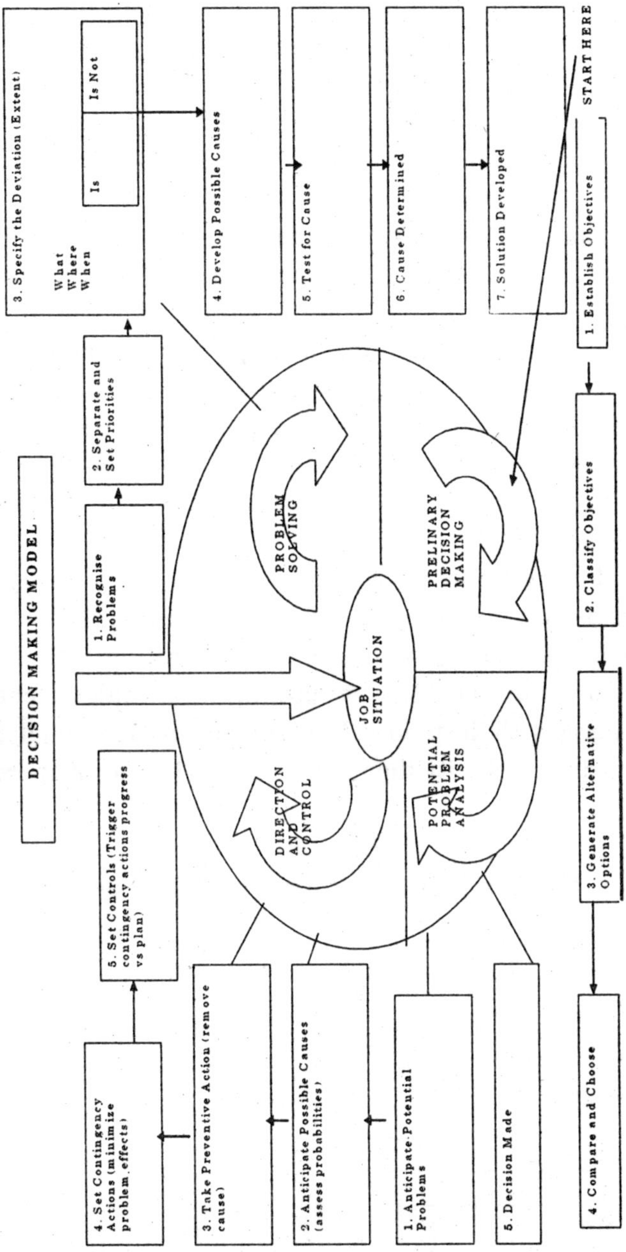

Source: Adapted from Kepner & Tregoe, 1981 and Fulmer, 1988, 99

Kepner and Tregoe (1981) have developed a graphic representation of the fact that decisions have somewhat cyclical nature. The exhibit demonstrates that managers should make more they know at which point in its cycle the problem situation is being encountered. The emphasis of this process is on a more rational approach designed to collect and make optional use of important pieces of information. (Fulmer: 1988)

The decision making model developed by Kepner and Tregoe (Exhibit 14) is a comprehensive one demonstrating job situation, covered mainly by four decision making related issues. These are primarily main steps in the process of rational decision making. Every major step has sequential minor steps, broadly divided into specific objectives and problems. Decision making is reflected not as one activity but a combination of all probable operational activities and thus making decision making as a management style.

It is very interesting that in public sector everything moves on paper and in a prescribed hierarchical order. The problem identified is sent to the lowest unit for analysis and suggesting alternatives. The upper ladder officials either agree or disagree with the proposal and recommend accordingly. The appropriate authority then put his stamp by way of approving

Exhibit 15

Decision Making Process in Public Sector

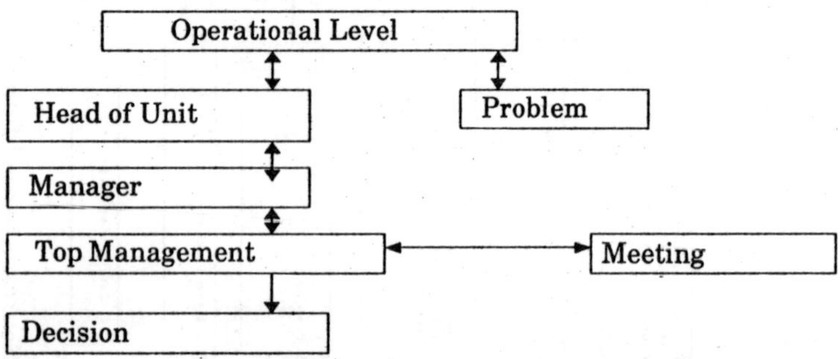

the proposal. (Exhibit 15) In few serious matters, problems are analysed in meetings and decisions are taken collectively, but responsibility lies solely with the top official presiding over the meeting. The general tendency is found to refer every matter to senior officials. Decisions in public sector are taken to solve the problems once they arise. There is no practice to identify problems and take preventive decisions before their occurrence. In this process a lot of time at every level is wasted. The decision making be delegated effectively and every level be made responsible for taking decisions in time.

Japanese Way of Decision Making

The only people who have developed a systematic and standardised approach to decision making are the Japanese. Their decisions are highly effective. Yet their approach violates every rule in the books on decision making. (Drucker :1974:465) It was effective time centred decisions taken by Japanese Industries during post-Second World War era which led the country to a level to which even developed countries felt jealous.

When the subject of decision making comes up with Japanese executives, the term 'ringi seido' or the 'ringi' system is invariably mentioned. It is a term used to describe a particular process of decision making widely used in large Japanese corporations. The word 'ringi' consists of two parts 'rin', meaning 'submitting a proposal to one's superior and receiving his approval', and 'gi' means 'deliberations and decisions'. The 'ringi' system has indeed all of these features. The basic philosophy of the 'ringi' system draws heavily on the process of decision making commonly employed in the traditional Japanese family system.

Under this system, authority and responsibilities for each level of management are not clearly defined. No policy guidelines are specified by top management. The system is based on decision making by group's participation and consensus. The

Exhibit 16
The Decision Making Sequence

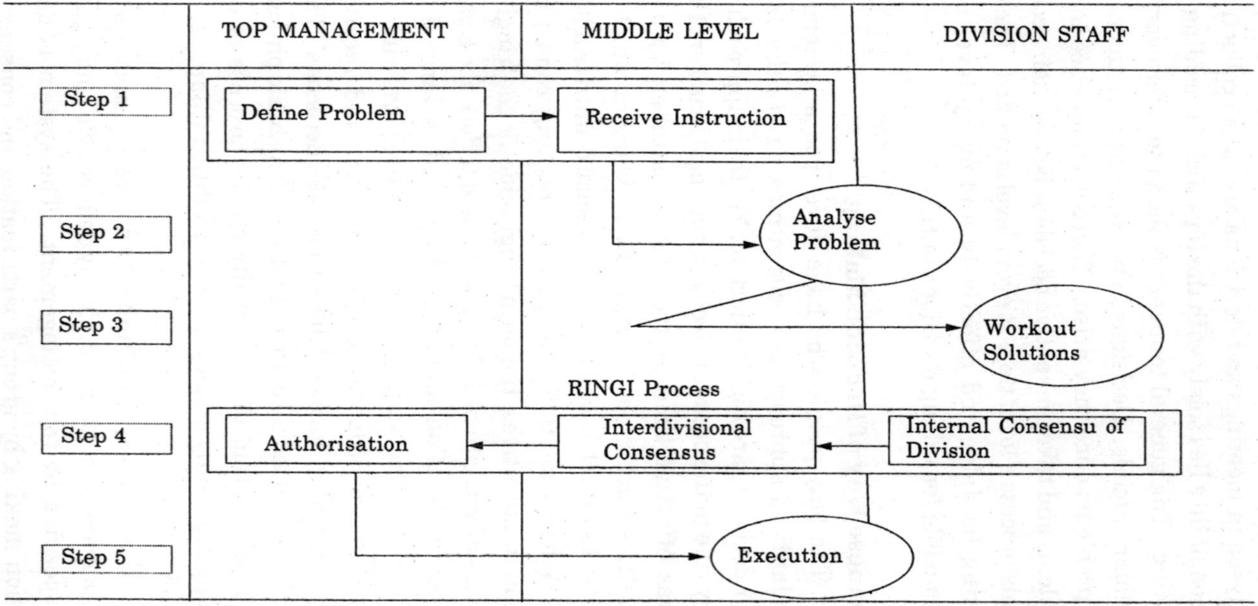

Source: Ichiro Hattori as adapted in Yoshino, 1981, 108

responsibilities for decision making are thus highly diffused and cannot be associated with any one individual. Furthermore, top management can only act on matters submitted by lower levels of management -it cannot itself initiate new ideas. Thus under the strict 'ringi' system, the role of the president of the company is, in effect, that of legitimizing decisions made by group consensus by affixing his seal of approval. Under this system, top management is not expected to exert strong leadership. (Yoshino: 1981:14)

Although it is a formalized process of group decision making, the 'ringi' system really reflects the inadequate definition of individual scope of action within a group. Efforts are now being made to revise or to abolish this system. The consequence is that the companies must clearly define the authority and responsibility attached to each position in their organisations, actively encourage individual decision making, precisely determine the relations between line and staff, and fully embrace modern methods of communication. Indeed, there is a growing recognition that the central problem of Japanese business organisation is its overwhelming need to establish a rational work structure and integrate it with the traditional human structure that already exists. (Takamiya : 1991)

'Ringi' may seem to be very democratic because all levels of management are involved in the decision making, but it can also become a convenient way of avoiding responsibility and therefore amounts to collective irresponsibility. There is no space on the decision forms to indicate disapproval. Sometimes 'ringi' is called a 'delegation of power to the top'. In the decision making process, it seems that the Japanese have a tendency to skip intermediate alternatives and relevant factors, and jump to one final conclusion. In other words, they short circuit between means and ends and arrive at the goal intuitively, and after such a goal has been defined it becomes the task of everyone concerned to work out various alternatives and means in order to arrive at a goal. Sometimes, the goal may not be appropriate, it may even be unrealistic. But it does not matter, since the main concern is the process of arriving at it, and not necessarily the accomplishment of the goal. (Imai & Norbury: 1981)

In sum, decision making is not a mechanical job. It is risk taking and a challenge to judgments. The right answer is not central. Central is understanding of the problem. Decision

Table 5.4
Decision Making by HRD Managers

(Percentage Distribution)

Factors	*Yes*		*No*	*Not Feasible*	*Employees Lack capability*	*Total*
	Great Extent	*Some Extent*				
Identify Problems individually	30	40	20	10	-	100
Develop alternatives	55	40	05	-	-	100
Making operational decisions	50	40	10	-	-	100
Making major decisions	5	10	15	70	-	100
Encourage employees to come with	5	15	10	30	40	100
Inviting views of employees	5	10	5	20	60	100
Associating subordinates in decision making	5	5	10	40	40	100
Decisions taken by consensus	5	5	5	85	-	100
Decisions imposed	25	40	35		-	100

making, further is not an intellectual exercise. It mobilises the vision, energies and resources of the organisation for effective action. (Drucker : 1974:480)

The HRD Managers are unanimous (Table 5.4) that policy decisions are framed by the government and other major decisions are taken by top management under the overall guidelines provided by the government for running the public sector enterprises. The managers are empowered only to take minor operational decisions which have no direct bearing on organisational objectives. The petty decisions are taken by managers just to facilitate the working of their respective units.

As regard areas in which managers can take decision, data (Table 5.5) highlight that HRD managers have authority to take decisions related to matters emanating at operational levels. The areas earmarked for their interventions are helpful in creating a conducive culture of working in the organisation. The managers are responsible for hiring suitable persons,

Table 5.5
Areas in Which Decisions can be Taken

(Percentage Distribution)

Activities	*YES*		*NO*	*Total*
	Great Extent	*Some Extent*		
Describing the jobs	30	60	10	100
Enriching the jobs	25	50	25	100
Procuring employees	20	35	45	100
Developing employees	35	45	20	100
Assessing Potential	70	25	5	100
Appraising Performance	70	25	5	100
Role Development	30	35	35	100
Problem solving	35	45	20	100
Redressal of grievances	30	55	15	100
Creating working environment	20	35	45	100
Settling conflicts	25	50	25	100
Promoting employees	30	50	20	100
Granting incentives	15	30	55	100

develop and orient them towards organisational working. The managers have little scope to decide monetary incentives, but they can recommend names for granting incentives. Non-monetary incentives can be given by them.

Thus the managers are responsible for making efforts to improve efficiency of employees at operational level. It is therefore a necessity that investments are made in individual employees. The managers should therefore allocate time to those activities which can help create proper working environment in the organisation wherein every individual has some role to play effectively and make advancements as per his potential.

Delegating Effectively

Delegation is far more than a mechanical process. Every act of delegation is rooted in the relationship that exists between the subordinate and his boss, the mutual confidence and respect they have for one another, the ideas and attitudes that each brings to the transaction, and the potential rewards and satisfactions that each perceives as coming from it.

Delegation is a process of job enrichment. The manager must resist a temptation to delegate things that he dislikes handling. No manager can delegate away his ultimate responsibility for what his subordinates do. The act of delegation is at once a vote of confidence in and a test of the subordinate. Both authority and autonomy must be granted in due course. Delegation can thus be thought of as a box surrounding a significant unit of work. On the four sides, defining the limits of the work are the walls of contribution, authority, autonomy, and accountability.

Delegation should not consist of a haphazard or discrete series of incidents. It should be a process of planned growth. The purpose of delegation is to strengthen the subordinate's managerial muscles, not to give him an occupational hernia.

Initially, the manager-leader fits the back to the burden and burden to the back. As subordinates grow in competence, he makes the challenges and tests more exacting. This planning process requires patience on the manager's part. A certain number of errors are to be anticipated since the goal is improvement. At the outset, the executive would be wise to keep his finger on the pulse of his subordinate's actions, though without intruding. As the subordinate proves himself, the superior can tactfully ease himself out of the picture allowing the subordinate to supervise himself. (Cribbin: 1972: 191-5)

Delegation of authority to subordinates commensurate with their responsibility calls for greater tact and sound judgment. His capacity for management is reflected in the successful accomplishment of work by others who have been delegated the corresponding responsibility. For delegation to be effective, uninterrupted flow of information between manager and his subordinates is must. (Aggarwala: 1984:61)

A manager can't be doing every one's work. If he is doing his subordinate's work just because he or she (subordinate) is inefficient, he is neither helping the organisation nor the subordinate; nor do even his own self. It is his responsibility to educate, train and improve his subordinates. Since they can't do it efficiently, so does it; then manager will continue piling up his own workload and they will continue piling up a serious liability on the organization. (Kharb: 2003:204)

Leading managers tend to have responsibilities for more work than they can possibly execute themselves. They need to delegate some of it to others, together with some of their own positional authority. The benefit of effective delegation is that it gives you more time to lead and manage, especially where the following factors are involved:

- Complex and difficult management tasks
- Novel business development
- Strategic opportunities

- Productivity and quality improvement
- Communication of vision and strategy
- Key staff appointments
- Staff development and training
- Spearheading marketing drives
- Staying close to major customers
- Getting out of the office and listening to people

It is an established fact that delegation reduces burden of manager and thus a lot of time out of committed time can be saved by him. The time thus saved can be utilised effectively and fruitfully some where else. It is noticed that most of the managers restrain from delegating their authority. Although they claim their willingness to delegate, the organisational culture, rules and inadequate capacity available with subordinates hinder them from doing so. It seems that managers believe in managing by authority and not by persuasion. They doubt the capacity and capability of their subordinates.

In absence of delegation, all the papers are piled at the desk of the managers and they remain all the time busy in routine work and dealing with the papers. Confidentiality is quoted as another reason for not delegating generously. It reflects the apathy of managers to share information with their subordinates. Such a practice corroborates the earlier observations (discussed in previous chapters) that most of the committed time of managers is eaten away either by routine paper work (unproductive work) or by time robbers. They on the other hand are compelled to perform office work at home.

Managers should therefore develop their subordinates, upgrade their skills and then practice delegation. Delegation of authority in many cases facilitates employees' development. Managers should act as a guide, philosopher and trainer to their subordinates. Managers should show full confidence in subordinates and help them develop. Training of personnel plays an important role in developing required skills in employees.

But in no case the managers should left subordinates un-controlled and un-supervised as responsibility lies on the managers. Responsibility is never delegated.

Table 5.6
Extent of Delegation by Managers

(Percentage Distribution)

Indicators	YES		NO	No Scope	Subordinates Not competent	Total
	Great Extent	Some Extent				
They practice delegation	10	15	20	15	40	100
Rules permit delegation	5	10	40	45	-	100
Believe in developing subordinates through delegation	15	35	50	-	-	100
They have been delegated authority	5	10	70	15	-	100
Employees are trustworthy	20	30	50	-	-	100
Employees are competent to handle responsibility	20	30	50	-	-	100

In sum, it is found that in public sector no one wants to take the responsibility in the light of strict rules and regulations. Even the delegated authority is used cautiously. Managers usually refer the matters to top management for decision. In this shifting of responsibility a lot of time is wasted at all levels causing overall loss to organisation. The managers need to be oriented that loss of time is loss of money as well, because organisation pays for every second.

References

Aggarwala, Dharma Vira (1984), Management, Deep & Deep, New Delhi

Drucker, Peter F. (1954), The Practice of Management, Harper & Row Publishers, New York

Drucker, Peter F. (1974), Management (Tasks, Responsibilities, Practices), Allied Publisher Pvt. Ltd., Bombay Pearson, Barrie (1988), Common Sense Time Management for Personal Success, Mercury Books, Livingstone Kharb, Col. Karan (2003), Made to Lead, Wisdom Tree, New Delhi

Albrecht, Karl (1978), Successful Management by Objectives,Prentice Hall Press, New York

Kepner, Charles H. and Tregoe, Benjamin B. (1981), The New Rational Manager, Princeton Research Press, Princeton Fulmer, Rober M. (1988), The New Management, Macmillan Pub. Co., New York

Cribbin, James J. (1988), The Management, Macmillan Pub. Co., New York

Hattori, Ichiro (1981), A Proposition on Efficient Decision Making in the Japanese Corporation, Columbia Journal of World Business Japanese Corporation, Columbia Journal of World

Yoshino, Michael T. (1981), Ringi Seido: Collective Decision Making in World Executive's Digest (ed), Management Japanese Style, Makali, Manila

Yoshino, Michael Y. (1960), Japan's Managerial System: Tradition and Innovation, MIT, Massachusetts

Takamiya, Surumu (1981), The Process Petrifield (I), in World Executive's Digest (Ed), Management Japanese Style, Makali, Manila, 117-119

Imai, Masaaki with Norbury, Paul (1981), The Process Petrified (II) in World Executive's Digest (Ed) Management Japanese Style, Makali, Manila, 120-1

Imai, Masaaki with Norbury, Paul (1975), The Japanese Businessman: An Introduction to his Behaviour & Business Strategy, Associated Business Programmes Ltd., London

Lakein, Alan (1973), How to Get Control of Your Time and Your Life, Signet, New York

Haimann, Theo, Scott, William G. and Connor, Patrick E. (1978), Managing the Modern Organization, Houghton Mifflin, Co., Boston

6

Managing Ownself

Introduction

With the advancing age and elevated positions in life, a person feels all the more constraints of time, because demand upon time increases and the available time is continually squeezed. The end of life even appears to be approaching and thereby one begins to feel importance of time all the more. Available time in every one's life is not unlimited; it is a finite resource-24 hours a day from birth to death. Time management i.e. life management is thus, in effect, management of self. Managing others is comparatively easier than managing the self because that requires cultivation of a sense of utmost discipline and self restraint.

Dru Scott (1998) says a self motivating flexible time management programme can only be obtained by combining time management techniques with an 'I love myself' philosophy. Her fundamental message is simple: "Like yourself, trust your gut instinct and cultivate your intensive soul which will enable you to create your own original ways." She advises to be 'real' and learn time management with ways uniquely tailored to suit one's own habits and needs, eliminating guilt and unrealistic perfectionism and using 'productive selfishness' to plan a day.

Punctuality

Punctuality is a one big aspect of time management. Mere reaching the place of work at the appointed time is very limited notion of punctuality. Punctuality, to be of value, must deliver. Value is added to it when a sense of punctuality is accompanied by commitment and loyalty. (Kharb: 2003)

The HRD Managers feel to be punctual in reaching office and attending the jobs. Many of them however have different opinion. They are of the view that reaching office at designated time and remaining in the office for all the time are not important. More important is the job one performs. Simple remaining in office is not going to help achieve the

Table 6.1
Level of Punctuality

(Percentage Distribution)

Factors	*Great Extent*	*Some Extent*	*Not at all*	*Total*
Punctual in reaching office	95	3	2	100
Punctuality as a mark of discipline	80	15	5	100
Punctual in attending office work	70	25	5	100
Punctual in household chores	60	20	20	100
Punctual in societal functions	40	30	30	100
Punctual in private life	30	40	30	100

organisational objectives. It seems that managers misinterpret the meaning of punctuality. Reaching office at the time fixed for the purpose is one indicator of punctuality. An employee should attend the jobs punctually as well. Punctuality is a mark of discipline. If a manager fails to be punctual, how can he direct his subordinates to be punctual?

The analysis (Table 6.1) depicts that managers are punctual to a great extent in reaching office, in attending office work and also in attending household chores but not much concerned about punctuality in societal functions as well as in private life. Even though absolute majority of respondents feel punctuality as a mark of discipline, the ambiguity in pattern of responses depicts the other side of the story. A man not much punctual in personal life cannot be punctual in public life. The incompatible response shows that managers see punctuality in a narrow sense. The spirit of punctuality seems to be belied. There is a need to adopt holistic view of punctuality.

Habits of Effectiveness

Parkinson's Law lays down that when works increase, time decreases and when works decrease, time increases. Hence the less important tasks have to be sacrificed for more important ones. Priorities are to be set. According to Management Guru Covey (1992), the 'seven habits' are habits of effectiveness. Because they are based on principles, they bring the maximum long-term beneficial results possible. They become the basis of a person's character, creating an empowering centre of correct maps from which an individual can effectively solve problems, maximise opportunities, and continually learn and integrate other principles in an upward spiral of growth. The effective habits, internalized principles and patterns of behaviour as developed by Covey are shown in Exhibit 17.

According to Covey (1992:85-86), the problems generally faced by an individual fall in one of three areas: direct control (problems involving our own behaviour), indirect control (problems involving other people's behaviour), or no control (problems we can do nothing about it). Direct control problems are solved by working on our habits. These are the Private Victories of Habits 1, 2 &3. Indirect control problems are solved by changing our methods of influence. These are Public Victories of Habits 4, 5&6. No control problems involve taking the responsibility to change the line on the bottom of our face – to smile, to genuinely and peacefully accept these problems and learn to live with them.

Thus, for managing themselves, managers should concentrate on habits related to Private Victories. These habits are: Be Proactive, Begin with the End in Mind, and Put first

Exhibit 17

The Seven Habits Paradigm

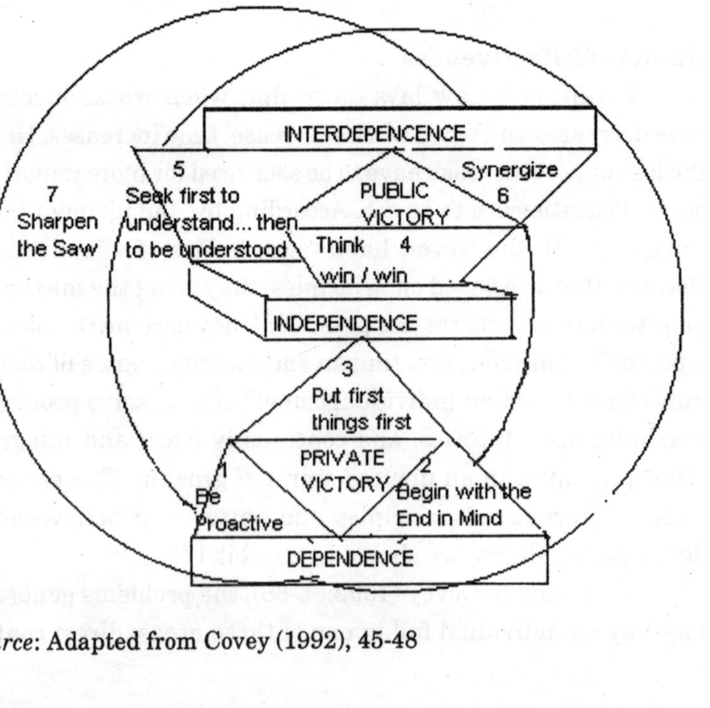

Source: Adapted from Covey (1992), 45-48

things First. According to Covey, the seventh habit, Sharpen the Saw, surrounds other habits on the Seven Habits Paradigm, because it is this habit that makes all the others possible. It is preserving and enhancing the greatest asset one has – 'me' (individual, you). It is renewing the four dimensions of our nature – physical, spiritual, mental and social/emotional.(Covey: 1992:287-8)

Every dimension of individual nature has certain instincts, which influence one's behaviour and life style. There are certain measures to achieve those dimensions and instincts. All these dimensions of nature are inter-related and influence each other. These are:

PHYSICAL – Exercise, Nutrition, Stress Management

MENTAL – Reading, Visualizing, Planning, Writing

SOCIAL/EMOTIONAL- Service, Empathy, Synergy, Intrinsic Security

SPIRITUAL – Value classification & commitment, Study & Meditation

As discussed earlier, each generation of time management builds on those that have preceded it, the strengths and some of the tools of each of the first three generations provide elemental material for the fourth, the latest one. But there is an added dimension which leads to become principle centred and to manage ourselves to do what is truly most important (i.e. activities falling in Quadrant II of Time Management Matrix, as discussed in earlier pages). The objective of Quadrant II management is to manage our lives effectively – from a centre of sound principles, from knowledge of our personal mission, with a focus on the important as well as the urgent. This is admittedly an ambitious objective for people caught in Quadrants III & IV. But striving to achieve it will have a phenomenal impact on personal effectiveness. (Covey: 1992: 160)

Thus, self management centres around the activities related to Quadrant II. Covey (1992) prescribes six important criteria need to be met by a Quadrant II organizers Managers should make every effort to devote more time on activities falling under this quadrant, the activities which are important but not urgent. To become a successful and effective Quadrant II organizer, managers should follow these rules.

Coherence

There must be harmony, unity and integrity between vision and mission, roles and goals, priorities and plans, desires and disciplines. The managers should have a personal mission statement and also a place for roles and for both short and long term goals. The roles of managers should be to achieve the goals set under the vision and mission of managers. For the purpose, they should prioritise activities and plan them. There must be coherence in this cycle.

Balance

True effectiveness requires balance, and the tool needs to help create and maintain it. The tool should help to keep balance in life, to identify various roles and keep them right in front, so that important areas such as health, family, professional preparation or personal development are not neglected. Managers should adopt holistic view of development. Neither success in official works should be a complete motto or the isolated attention on personal life. There must be a balance between official life and personal life. No dimension deserves neglect by managers.

Important and Urgent Focus

A tool should encourage, motivate and actually help in spending the time needed in Quadrant II, so that prevention is dealt rather than crises are prioritised. While planning the day or week, the key is not to prioritize what's on the schedule, but to schedule priorities. Managers should not limit themselves to plan the activities before them, but they should first prioritise the activities and then plan their accomplishment. They should not wait for emerging the crisis (urgency), rather they should plan the activities in a such a way that there remains remote scope for occurrence of any crisis. They should therefore identify important tasks and plan for their performance.

A People's Dimension

The tool should deal with people and not just schedules. Efficiency is concerned in dealing with time, a principle-centered person thinks in terms of effectiveness in dealing with people. The tool needs to reflect that value, to facilitate implementation rather than create guilt when a schedule is not followed. While preparing a time management plan, manager should remember that the plan is to deal with the human being. It should have value added focus. Plan should catalyse implementation. It should be worth followed.

Flexibility

Planning should be servant, never a master. Planning should be tailored to style, needs, and particular ways. The time plan charted out by managers should not be a rigid tool. It should be flexible enough with a scope of providing cushion to urgency, problems, crisis etc. Plan should not be a mechanism to control the managers but managers should have full control over it. The rigid planning hinders accomplishment; hence managers should often avoid it.

Portability

Tool should be portable, so that one can carry it with most of the time. The time planner adopted by managers should be simple and short. It should be easily understandable and implement able. Managers should always carry their planner for better appreciation of their planning utility.

Since Quadrant II is the heart of effective self management, a tool should help move into Quadrant II. If managers keep these principles in mind while developing their time management planning schedule, they will be able to be effective manager.

In the circumstances it is of importance to be aware of the perception of managers, on one hand, and highlight the real perspective of personal habits, on the other.

Table 6.2
Traits of Managers

(Percentage Distribution)

Measures	*Yes*	*No*	*Total*
Habits are personal property	95	5	100
Habits shape personality	80	20	100
Habits have bearing on efficiency	40	60	100
Habits influence our life	70	30	100
Habits can be altered/refined	30	70	100
Habits design values of life	50	50	100
Habits create attitude	60	40	100
Habits are strengths	25	75	100

Many of the managers feel that habits being personal traits have nothing to do with their effectiveness. But they fully recognize the role of habits in shaping the personality of an individual. But they are found aware of the importance of habits

(Table 6.2). Managers do recognize the importance of habits on life and personality development, but they do not relate it with their efficiency and strengths. Habits are personal traits which affect one's efficiency and perception about life. It has a direct bearing on managing one's time, thus shaping the life.

Table 6.3
Measures Adopted for Managing Personal Time

(Percentage Distribution)

Activities	*Yes*	*No*	*Total*
Recognise various dimension of life	70	30	100
Adopt measures to meet requirements of dimensions	40	60	100
Go on walks	85	15	100
Practice yoga	30	70	100
Do exercise at home	40	60	100
Attend gyms	20	80	100
Go to swimming pools	10	90	100
Recreation clubs	15	85	100
Meditation	35	65	100
Religious activities	55	45	100
Use piece of paper to record priorities	20	80	100
Use diaries/planners	35	65	100
Memorise	15	85	100

In regard to classify their life in four dimensions as suggested by Covey, it is illustrated that many of the managers have informal arrangements to meet a few requirements of dimensions. Some go for walks, few others practice 'yoga', 'pranayam' etc. and a few attend recreation clubs and gyms. As regards prioritising their activities, it is found that some managers note down their priorities either on a piece of paper or on a pocket diary or use an electronic diary. But they lack scientific knowledge of managing their time. They just record the engagements to keep them on time and be punctual in fulfilling their engagements.

Becoming a Self Manager

Self organisation involves four key activities. These are identifying roles, selecting goals, scheduling, and daily adapting. (Covey: 1992:162) The first task is to write down roles. Everyone has a role as an individual, role as a family member, a few roles in work, indicating different areas in which time and energy are invested on a regular basis. The nature of roles/should be confined to a day or a week. The next step is to think two or three important results proposed to be accomplished in each role during the next seven days. These would be recorded as goals. Some of these activities should reflect important activities. Ideally, these short-term goals would be tied to the long-term goals identified in conjunction with mission statement.

Having identified roles and set goals, one can translate each goal to a specific day of the week on the priority basis based on four human dimensions (as discussed earlier). Daily planning becomes more a function of daily adapting, of prioritizing activities and responding to unanticipated events, relationships, and experiences in a meaningful way. The whole exercise is sequenced in the Exhibit 18.

The only way to discover strengths is through feedback analysis. Practiced consistently, this simple method shows within a fairly short period of time, where strengths lie. Several implications for action follow from feedback analysis. First and foremost, managers should concentrate on strengths. Second,

Exhibit 18
Managing Self

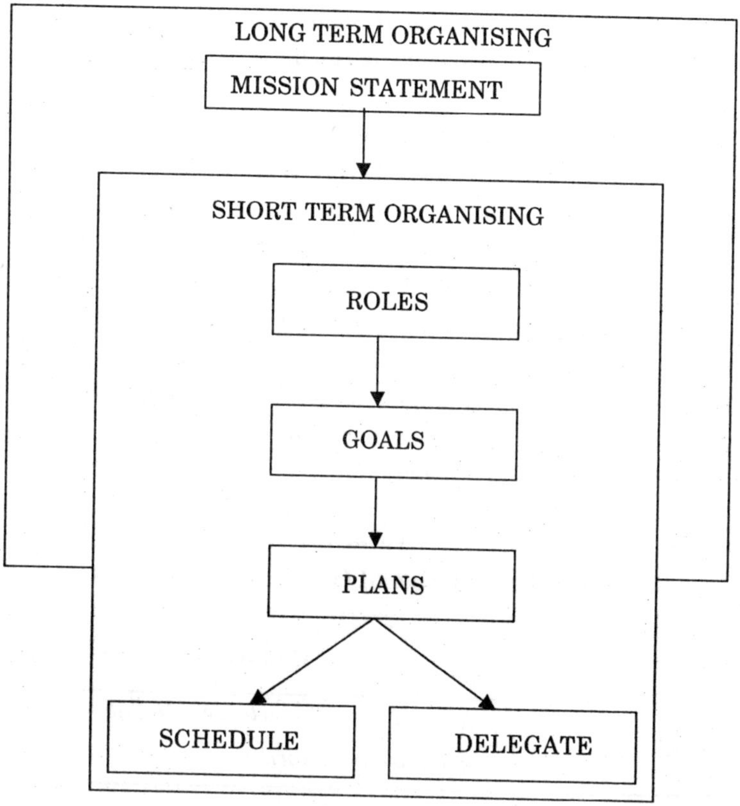

Source: Adapted from Covey (1992), 168

they should work on improving strengths. Analysis will rapidly show where one needs to improve skills or acquire new skills. It will also show the gaps in one's knowledge – and those can usually be filled. Thirdly, they should discover where their intellectual arrogance is causing disabling ignorance and managers overcome it.

For too many people, especially people with great expertise in one area, or contemptuous of knowledge in other areas or believe that being bright is a substitute for knowledge. Human resource professionals often pride themselves on their ignorance of elementary accounting or of quantitative methods altogether. But taking pride in such ignorance is self defeating. Like one's strengths, how one performs is unique. It is a matter of personality.

Organisations, like people, have values; to be effective in an organisation, the manager's values must be compatible with the organization's values. They do not need to be the same, but they must be close enough to co-exist. Otherwise, the manager will not only be restricted but will also not produce results.

A manager's strengths and the way he performs rarely conflict; the two are complementary. But there is sometimes a conflict between a manager's values and his or her strengths. In that case, the work may not appear to be worth devoting one's life to. (Drucker: 1999)

Table 6.4

Have Knowledge of Other Departments

(Percentage Distribution)

Indicators	*Level of Satisfactory*	*Knowledge Normal*	*Not at all*	*Total*
Have knowledge of finances/audit	15	30	55	100
Acquaint with sales/marketing	10	20	70	100
Know the production level	10	25	65	100
Have knowledge of market	5	10	85	100
Aware of internal environment	10	15	75	100
Have knowledge of external environment	5	10	85	100

Surprisingly, a little number of HRD Managers have knowledge of other departments of their organisation. Unfortunately in the name of specialization and professionalism, managers today are squeezing their knowledge. A good time manager irrespective of his specific work field should have complete knowledge of his surroundings. In absence, his time planning activities may fail to produce desired effectiveness.

HRD Managers to be effective should have knowledge of the whole organisation he serves with and all activities and have additional specific knowledge about human resources. The knowledge of other units may help them procure the suitable man-power and develop human resources accordingly.

Controlling the Use of Time

The most valuable resource the managers have is their own time. To make more effective use of their time, they must (i) determine how they spend their time, (ii) analyse how they use their time, (iii) set priorities and develop a time use strategy, and (iv) implement an effective time plan. (Glueck: 1980)

Managers consistently over-estimate the time devoted to production and underestimate the time spent on other matters. The first step toward better control of their time is to learn how to use time now. Only through recording and observational methods can they do this effectively.

Analysing How to Use Time

Time analysis can be done in several ways. The first way is to total the categories and see how much time is spent in various activities such as personal time, telephone calls, conferences and individual discussions. Then manager can examine how he allocates time to functional areas and analyse the flow of activities. This includes a study of the time taken up by interruptions. Next, time can be divided into four categories: creative, preparatory, productive and overhead. Creative time is time devoted to planning future activities, new product ideas and the like. Preparatory time is time spent in setting up activities such as gathering facts in preparation for a conference. Productive time is time spent actually doing the job. Overhead time is time spent on correspondence and reports, paperwork, public relations, and so forth.

The managers are found spending lot of time at home also on phone calls. Many managers use personal time for office work even while they have no shortage of time during committed hours. This happens because lack of planning of jobs and allocating time at office as well as at home. Most time of managers is spent as overhead time.

Setting Priorities and Developing a Time Use Strategy

Time is divided into several categories: work, pleasure, sleep, personal hygiene, self development, travel etc. Managers should set personal priorities among these categories. Allocation of time is a reflection of one's life style, beliefs and attitudes. The importance of setting priorities should be evident as 80 per cent of results come from the vital 20 per cent of activities. Managers are found neither prioritising their activities nor allocating time, hence a complete mess.

Implementing an Effective Time Plan

A basic element of effective time management is developing a time budget for a week or a day. Every manager has to spend roughly 10 hours daily (on all working days) on matters related to office. This consists of eight hours of working hours and two hours on travel etc. Although managers express to spend one hour on travel and eight hours in office they are skeptical. Some times they are supposed to go early and many a times over stay in office. Hence for analysis purpose ten hours have been taken into account as office hours and remaining fourteen hours as personal ones.

Table 6.5
Time Allocated on Personal Activities

Activities	*Time spent (mts/day) working days*	*Extra time spent on Sunday (hrs)*	*Time spent (hrs/week) (7 days)*	*Proportion of daily personal time (14 hrs)*	*Proportion of total personal time (108 hrs)*	*Pro-portion of 24 hrs.*
Morning walk	30		3.5	3.6	3.24	2.1
Evening walk	30		3.5	3.6	3.24	2.1
Personal hygiene	60	1	8.00	7.1	7.41	4.2
Reading newspapers, magazines etc.	30		3.5	3.6	3.24	2.2
Eating	60	1	7.00	7.1	6.5	4.2
Watching TV programmes	60		7.0	7.1	6.5	4.2
Paid recreation (including outing)		4	4.00	7.1	3.79	
Guiding children	30		3.5	3.6	3.24	2.1
Attending visitors (average)	30	1	4.5	3.6	4.17	2.1

(Contd.)

(Contd. Table 6.5)

Activities	*Time spent (mts / day) working days*	*Extra time spent on Sunday (hrs)*	*Time spent (hrs / week) (7 days)*	*Proportion of daily personal time (14 hrs)*	*Proportion of total personal time (108 hrs)*	*Pro-portion of 24 hrs.*
Phone calls	30		3.5	3.6	3.24	4.2
Disposing office works	30		3.5	3.6	3.24	2.1
Shopping/marketing	-	2	2.0		1.85	-
Visiting friends etc. (average)	30	1	4.5	3.6	4.17	2.1
Planning household	30	-	3.5	3.6	3.24	2.1
Chorus						
Day rest	30	1	4.5	3.6	4.17	2.1
Sleep	6hrs.		42.0	42.85	38.89	25.0
Total	14 hrs		108.0			

Thus a manager has at least 14 hours at his own disposal. He can spend that time as he deems fit. In respect of pattern of use of this time, the analysis depicts a little amount of time used by managers on physical and mental dimensions. In the present era of stress and strain, managers should keep themselves healthy – physically as well as mentally. If they lose their health, nothing can compensate that loss. The managers should allocate time for all dimensions to maintain balance in life. Further, managers were desired to plan jobs and not the priorities even at home where they are the masters of their time. Unless and until priorities are set, time cannot be used effectively and fruitfully.

Time Out from Tension

Modern society has undergone rapid technological progress and the industry has played an integral part in this change process. Like the rest of the society, the industrial world has had to adjust behaviourally to both the beneficial and the deleterious effects of a fast pace and a pressured life. These behavioural adjustments are emotionally and physiologically stressful, and they lead to undesirable effects on health and well being. (Peters & Benson: 1978:120) Elevated blood pressure resulting from stress is perhaps the major predisposing factor in the development of heart attacks and strokes. (Gutmann & Benson: 1971:543) Excessive mental irritability and anxiety are still other common manifestations of stress.

There is a very simple way for many individuals to deal with stress and thus to prevent it or at least control many of its damaging effects: to elicit 'the relaxation processes'. This is an innate physiological reaction, characterized by decreases in metabolic rate, heartbeats, and breathing rate. A person can bring forth the relaxation response by practicing any one of a number of simple techniques. Investigations have demonstrated, however, that the relaxation response may be elicited by various techniques as well. Four elements common to all these techniques are a relatively quiet environment, a comfortable position, a repetitive mental stimulus, and a passive attitude. (Benson: 1975)

The data (Table 6.5) reveal that managers are not allocating adequate time for activities which are helpful in reducing stress and strain. Many managers go for walk on medical advice. If an individual pay attention on mental and spiritual dimensions and allocate some time for the related activities, tension can be reduced. Meditation is the best way to beat the stress. Meditation is always associated with a serene mind and a quiet atmosphere. Twenty-thirty minutes of meditation daily will also increase resistance to stress.

Meditation improves memory, listening abilities as well as teaches patience and resistance. Meditation starts with simple breathing. Just two-three minutes of deep breathing immediately helps in reducing stress of any kind while regular deep breathing immunize one from mental illness. The best form of meditation is chanting. Managers should close their eyes, sit with legs crossed and chant 'om' for 15-20 seconds and open eyes slowly. In this way they can reduce stress and strain to a great extent.

Commuter Time

During the last few decades, the field of study connected with the economics of time that has attracted most attention is almost certainly that of the value of transport time savings. Time saving values used to guide investment or planning decisions must, it is apparent, relate to average values based on a high degree of aggregation. Empirical evidence suggests that the average traveller would receive different amounts of utility from the same time period spent travelling by different transport modes.

All other things being equal, they would therefore value a reduction in journey times in a less preferred mode more highly than the same reduction in the journey time in a more favoured transport mode. If work time journeys are shortened and if the time saved can be used productively, then society will gain the total value of the increased production. (Bruzelius: 1979)

The journey to and from work is one of the most important forms of travel. Many factors affect each individual commuter's evaluation of the amount of utility that he will gain if he is able to transfer time from his commuting journey to some preferred activity. Reductions in travel-to-work times will only have any value if there is some alternative activity available that is more attractive than travelling. A particular feature of commuting time savings is that they occur on days when the stock of time available for non-paid work activities is relatively small.

Time savings cannot be transferred from one day to another but must normally be consumed when they are made. The exact time when some new 'free' time becomes available can be varied by rearranging other non-paid-work activities but it would be impracticable to move free time from a holiday or a week end to a working day. Apart from the suggestion that people allocate a fairly fixed amount of time to commuting, there is a more general hypothesis that states that individuals have a fixed time budget for all travel purposes.

The amount of time allocated to travelling depends on a complex interaction between free choice and necessity. One important influence on the travel-time choices that are available is the decision by individual about the way he will live. This decision will itself be influenced by attitudes towards travelling time. Commuting costs consist of both money costs and time costs. There is a stronger case for believing that the unit value of time is constant for non-work time savings.

Time saved from commuting journeys, for example, does not need to be used for any particular productive purpose in order to have value. Spending time at home doing 'nothing' in particular may be considered preferable to using the same time on a commuter journey. For non-work journeys, where the preferences of the traveller, rather than the value of lost output, determine time saving values, it might be expected that small time savings would have more value on shorter journeys.(Sharp: 1981)

It can be seen from data analysed in previous pages that managers use (waste) a lot of time in commuting. Daily commuting between residence and office consumes about six hours weekly. Many managers use official car, hence their commuting time is usually free time. Managers can devote this time for calling back on telephones, reading newspapers/ magazines, planning, thinking, reviewing day's plan etc. In addition, managers generally spend many hours per week in traveling to markets, visiting friends, meeting social commitments etc. The managers can plan this time for better and fruitful use. Commuting time can be used for meditation, dhyan, yoga etc. These will help ease tension and stress.

Leisure Time

As discussed earlier, it is possible to divide time into two categories: work time and non-work time, and all non-work time is sometimes, described as leisure time. In his general theory of the economics of time, De Serpa (1971:834) argues that the essential nature of leisure was that the time consumption constraint is ineffective and that when people choose to allocate more time to the consumption of goods than is required then these become 'leisure goods'.

In The Price of Leisure, Owen (1970:3) develops the definition of leisure as time spent in consumption, consumption time itself being defined as time devoted to activities which are, at the margin, primarily carried on for their own sake rather than for the control over financial or other resources which the activity might yield. According to Owen, this definition excludes paid work, housework, and do-it yourself repairs and commuting time but includes sleeping and eating time. Owen discusses an alternative definition of leisure time as "free time" that could be devoted to recreation and non-productive contemplation.

Vickerman, in his book The Economics of Leisure and Recreation (1975), is mainly concerned with planning to meet recreational needs and he has a much wider definition of leisure as any activity that can take place in leisure time. His definition would include the journey to work and shopping and presumably, housework and do-it yourself activities. Vickerman has an interesting sub-division of leisure time into three categories: recreation, pleasure and social activities. He uses the term 'recreation' to cover organised activities such as entertainment, sport and eating out. He also subdivides recreation into market recreation, where the primary activity is commercially marketed (cinema, professional sport) and non-market recreation, which is not sold in saleable units. Pleasure relates to activities that are not organised commercially, such as holidays, while he defines social activities as 'essentially involving people and not places', the primary purpose being to visit friends.

All these activities yield some level of positive or negative utility. The chief characteristic of pure leisure activities is that they must be undertaken 'for their own sake' because they produce only direct utility. All activities that produce some indirect benefit that will be enjoyed in a future time period may be classified as relating to work or non-leisure time. Paid work is a special case of work activity. Activities producing indirect utility are not always undertaken primarily in order to enjoy their future benefit.

It is possible to develop a classification of activities based either on economic factors or on psychological motivation. Those activities that lead to the output of some goods or service could be classified as being productive. These could be subdivided into those where the product is marketed and those where is not. The first category of productive activities with marketed products would include all paid work and travel to, from and in the course of work. Productive activities with non-marketed products would include housework, do-it yourself activities, gardening, keeping animals, education and child care.

Consumption activities could be subdivided into those involving measurable marginal costs such as eating, pleasure travel and visits to the hairdresser, and those that require market goods inputs but for which marginal costs per time period are very low, such as sleeping, sports and walking for pleasure.

Although free time in which recreational and other pleasurable activities can take place is generally regarded as being desirable, in fact there seem to be at least two problems. One is the expected future shortage of paid work and the consequent surplus amount of leisure time that will become available. The second problem relates to the use that can be made of the growing amounts of leisure time and the readiness with which the economy can be adapted to provide the goods inputs required for recreational activities. (Sharp: 1981)

The data (table 6.5) show that a lot of time is available with the managers which are surely for not paid work and may be termed as leisure time or free time. The managers should judiciously use the leisure time available because the better use of free time may help reduce tension in life and bring freshness after every break.

Achieving Balance in Life

Every one needs to achieve some degree of balance in his life otherwise he may achieve his success goals only to find he has lost what he belatedly discovers is more important to him.

Time management used effectively means that managers will not just find time, but plan time, for the things which are essential for them to enjoy success.

For achieving balance in life the managers should allocate time for activities related to all dimensions of life. They should spare some time daily for exercise to help reduce tension of today's fast life; they should be concerned about eating and sleeping. They should go for recreation and outing. The managers should reserve some time for their family. Thus they should plan a balanced life.

Table 6.6
Emphasis on Balanced Life

(Percentage Distribution)

Activities	*Great Extent*	*Some Extent*	*Not*	*Total*
Time spend on Reading (other than newspapers)	15	35	50	100
Time spent on writing	5	10	85	100
Time spent on visualizing	5	15	80	100
Time spent on planning	10	20	70	100
Time spent on meditation	5	10	85	100
Time spent on exercise	10	25	65	100
Time spent on recreation	30	40	30	100
Time spent on outing	15	20	65	100
Time spent on societal activities	25	30	45	100

The managers seem to maintain a balance in their life but unconsciously and in totally ad-hoc manner. They need to spend more time on planning and visualizing. These activities bring creativity. Reading and writing develop knowledge and preparedness. The managers should adopt holistic views towards life. Only material achievement is not a way to a balanced life.

Getting Healthy

This requires managers to pay attention of what they eat and drink. Equally important, they must plan and make time available for exercise and relaxation. If health suffers, their success may simply lead to bitterness. Most of the managers pay attention towards their health and hygiene. Managers believe to have nutritious food and enriched break fast.

Table 6.7
Attention of Health and Relaxation

(Percentage Distribution)

Activities	*Satisfactory*	*Normal*	*Medical Advice*	*Total*
Have nutritious food	60	20	20	100
Particular about balanced diet	50	30	20	100
Devote time on exercise	30	40	30	100
Take complete rest	60	30	10	100
Enjoy free time	70	30	-	100
Visit gyms	30	60	10	100
Go for swimming	10	80	10	100
Meditation , Yoga	65	30	15	100

Attending Family and Friends

It is so easy to enjoy work so much and to focus so much on success goals that managers feel they don't really need to spend much time to their family. They are providing them with plenty of money to do the things they enjoy. Managers should not befool themselves. The gift family and friends value and appreciate most is spending time with them.

Something to consider in order achieving balance in life is to get managers involved with helping the community or working for a charity. If they can choose an activity which they can be involved in with members of their family, so much is the better. (Pearson: 1988:18-19)

It is surprising that many managers express to spend free time with family. They seem to be confused between free time used by them in relaxing or recreation and give exclusive time to parents, wife, children, sisters, brothers and other friends. They say all the time beyond office hours is spent with family and friends. They have nothing for themselves. The need of the hour is that managers should allocate time exclusively for each role of theirs. Family members deserve some time spent exclusively with the head of the family who is a principal earning member and guardian of the family.

Table 6.8
Time for Family and Friends

(Percentage Distribution)

Variables	*Yes*	*No*	*Total*
Have some exclusive time for family	30	70	100
Go for outing with family	60	40	100
Spend time with children	70	30	100
Spare time for social / community activities	40	60	100

It is therefore suggested that managers should look into their time budget regularly and critically whether it is being spent properly. There should be time specified for every task and they should develop a habit to attend it timely. If the time is managed well, indeed then, work does not remain work-load, rather becomes pleasure. They should begin daily life with quiet time for thinking, prioritising etc. A word of caution is not out of place for utmost time conscious and busy managers as they are the lot most prone to blood pressures, tension, nervous breakdown and the like.

To counter the 'fastness' achieved as a result of time management, HRD managers should learn to relax, know about healthy effects of healthful living, exercise, laughing, singing, dancing, pranayam, silence, meditation, dhyan etc., and practice them as and when need arises and at leisure and pleasure rather than making them integral part of their living and address themselves perpetually, "what is the best use of my time right now at this moment". (Bajaj: 1998: 39-40)

References

Bajaj, B.L. (1998), Time Management, Prashasnika, XXV (1), January – June, 33-40

Scott, Dru as quoted in Bajaj, B.L. (1998), Time Management, Prashasnika, XXV (1), January-June, 36

Covey, Stephen R. (1992), The Seven Habits of Highly Effective People, Simon & Schuster, London

Drucker, Peter F. (1999), Managing Ourself, Harvard Business Review, March-April, 65-74

Glueck, W.F. (1980), Management, The Dryden Press, Illinois, App.18.1

Gutmann, Mary C. and Benson, Herbert (1971), Interaction of Environmental Factors and Systemic Arterial Blood Pressure: A Review, Medicine, November

Benson, Herbert (1975), The Relaxation Response, Morrow, New York

Peters, Ruanne K. and Benson, Herbert (1978), Time out from Tension, Harvard Business Review, January-February, 120-124

Sharp, Clifford (1981), The Economics of Time, John Wiley & Sons, New York

Kharb, Col. Karan (2003), Made to Lead, Wisdom Tree, New Delhi

Bruzelius, Nilb (1979), The Value of Travel Time, Croom Helm, London

De Serpa, A.C. (1971), A Theory of the Economics of Time, Economic Journal, December

Owen, J.D. (1970), The Price of Leisure, McGill Queen's University Press, Montreal

Vickerman, R.W. (1975), The Economics of Leisure and Recreation, Macmillan, London

Pearson, Barrie (1988), Common-Sense Time Management for Personal Success, Mercury Books, Livingsto

7

Epilogue

Human Resource Formation

Every organisation has three basic components: human (manpower), finance (money) and inventory (material). The optimum use of fiscal and material resources depends upon human resource. It is the human resource which is capable of making best use of other resources. Thus the efficiency of any organisation is linked with the human capital available with it. This has been realised, of course belatedly that the main factor behind the flourishing of private sector in the country has been the recognition of importance of human resource available. Now, the public sector enterprises have started taking a clue and are recognising the importance of human resource as an important 'capital' and are putting the 'human capital' at the highest pedestal.

The new economic policy, as enunciated by the Government of India since last decade of the twentieth century, has facilitated liberalisation, privatisation and globalisation. An era of competitiveness is emerging and the human resource available with public sector has to adapt to the new situation. The rapid and steady increase in population and a notable rise in literacy have led to abundance of human resource in the country. Unfortunately, until recent past, public sector has failed to recognise the importance of their manpower. Government being the biggest employer has been pursuing the welfare mode but now the scenario is changing fast. The post-liberalization era has destined an important role for human capital available to public sector in the country, thus now more emphasis on human development and human resource development. There is a paradigm shift in the area of human capital formation and its optimisation.

Time: an important resource

Time has been a major factor for influencing the efficiency and effectiveness of human capital and the organisation. There is a close relationship between the economic growth and industrial advancement and the importance attached to time. The managers in the post-liberalised economic era have to adopt a changed mind-set and understand value of time. Productive use of human resource is the main function of modern enterprises. Thus time is being recognised as an additional dimension of modern management system.

Time is a unique resource available to mankind. It is a fixed resource. It can neither be reduced nor increased. It is uniformly available to all and sundry. It depends on human capital whether to spend time usefully or uselessly. The time once lost is lost forever. The lost time cannot be retrieved. Time neither can be stored nor stopped. It passes unabatedly, without any rest or pause.

There are varied views regarding time. Some experts argue that passage of time is an important metaphysical act, while others feel the flow of time an illusion. The existence of a social system in any case necessitates some organisation of time. The focus always remains on alternate use of time. However, time has always been a subject of prime importance for economists. Every economic activity is linked with time. All the financial transactions centre on time. The cost of raw materials, value of product and operational cost, the whole manufacturing, procurement and marketing process contain time as an important factor. The post-Second World War Japan realised the importance of time; and it was the time factor which helped Japan achieve a rapid industrial advancement in a few decades only.

Management 'gurus' across the world having taken a clue from economists as well as from industrial development in Japan, have realized the importance of time. Since managerial functions are performed on decision making which in turn has a close link with time factor, time has now acquired the status of an additional dimension of management.

Effective Time Management

The pace of industrial development and emerging market competitiveness have led to a feeling of scarcity of time by everyone whereas periodicity of time remains fixed as 24 hours per day for all, neither less nor more .The new economic policy has created an era of competitiveness, and time has become the most important tool in the changing perspective. Time is also a crucial factor in managerial decision making. This requires an efficient system of utilisation of time, and such a system is known as time-cycle. Shorter the time- cycle, more are the opportunities to learn from experiences and make improvements. Managers should hence attempt to manage their time.

The time may be classified as: committed time or fixed time and personal time. Committed time indicates the periodicity of time fixed for office work. Personal time is the time beyond the office hours. There may be leisure time or free time. But all sorts of time cumulatively make 24 hours a day or 1440 minutes per day or 86400 seconds per day.

Managers have to perform a number of works at office as well as at home. Hence budgeting the time is an important tool for managing the time either at the office or at home. Use of time and allocation of time are affected by many factors. These factors may be related to person, role, resource and environment. Personal factors such as sex, age are the basic factors to be taken into account while allocating the time for different tasks either at office or at home. Employment and its nature, marriage and parenthood are other personal factors which affect time budgeting. Role factors are basically concerned with the official responsibilities. Resources include income and home technology and environmental factors consist of societal scheduling or ecological location. All these sets of factors mutually interact with one another. These factors affect the pattern of use of time.

Data collection on time-use is a pre-requisite for time budgeting. It has been observed that HRD Managers do not maintain any record of their time use. They however do keep the engagement schedule. There is no proper mechanism to allot time to each and every activity. If there is any allocation it is based on past experience. For lack of time budget, HRD Managers have no systematic planning of their day.

There are many public sector enterprises whose HRD Managers do prioritise their tasks but generally on the basis of urgency and not always on the criterion of importance. Their priority is disturbed because of urgency in many matters including orders from the senior bosses. There is always possibility of urgent orders from higher ups, but in absence of any systematic planning the whole day of HRD Managers is disturbed. The pre-planning may provide cushion to urgency and urgent orders from top brass.

The non-planning of the day as well as non-prioritising the tasks leaves many HRD Managers with plenty of compulsory idle time. The managers have to remain in office during the period fixed for working but the actual time spent on working is generally much less. Thus many managers have to eat their committed time almost daily. A systematic planning, prioritising the tasks and allocation of time for every activity may help in this regard. Their compulsory ideal time may be reduced and managers may plan its use for better purposes.

It has been observed that a good part of managers' time is spent on holding meetings or attending meetings, doing routine paper works, making telephone calls or receiving telephone calls, attending visitors etc. These subsidiary activities are of maintenance nature. These are necessary for getting informations, monitoring the performance, planning, making decisions etc. These activities form part of their duties. If planned, these activities help in productive use of their time.

It is observed that managers maintain engagement diaries for meetings and other important tasks and they often realise the wasteful expenditure of time on these activities, but they have to cope with the system. They have no control over these activities and moreso, they don't plan them, and most of the time these activities become time robbers or time wasters. Managers cannot avoid them, but plan them. If planned properly, these tasks help; if not planned, these become burden. The managers should therefore plan their main tasks, allot the time for each task and these maintenance activities can be placed suitably in the unallocated time.

Managers are found spending more time on maintenance activities like taking feedback, giving feedback, follow up unfinished jobs, vending visits, consultation, desk works etc. but they fail to allot adequate time on planning - planning the day, planning the tasks, planning the time, planning the job responsibilities, planning the future. No planning or no systematic planning results into chaos and crises and creates problems at implementation level; and this results into managers fighting the fire most of the time.

Managers should therefore take time for planning. For the purpose, they should prepare list of tasks prepared to be undertaken, then prioritise them on the basis of importance and urgency, allocate time to each activity and set deadlines and stick to it. Managers should identify their prime time and make best use of that time for most important works. They should learn to make decisions, they should take decisions and delegate decision making effectively. It has been observed that public sector offices are run through papers. Managers have to go through piles of papers. Hence they should handle any paper only once. They should avoid generating paper works, because more paper works create problems for others and also for themselves. Instead of paper work managers should make use of telephone for effective and speedy communication.

Managing time is not a new phenomenon. People have been managing, unconsciously, their time since days immemorial. In early days some people had strong memory, hence they memorised their priorities. Many others took the help of note books and checklists. This was the beginning of time management process. It was succeeded by use of calendars, planners, diaries, engagement pads etc. for keeping a tap on time. The third generation of time management brought use of electronic calendars, diaries, etc. The latest version of measures to manage control of time are personal computers, palm computers, lap tops etc. But all the four generations of time management are mutually linked and are inter- connected. They overlap each other. All the tools are used simultaneously.

The emergence of latest generation of time management however is not confined to use of electronic tools but has also given a new focus to the whole issue of time management. In earlier exercises, managers used to have time allocated for engagements as well as for the important or urgent works to be performed. But now the issue of time management has acquired new face lift. The management experts have linked time with life. Now, the focus is that by managing time, life is managed, the effective time management can lead to better quality of life. It has been found by studies that 80 per cent of productivity is achieved by 20 per cent of effective time of managers.

The effective time management per-supposes the identification and listing of tasks proposed to be performed by the managers during the day or the week. It has been realised through studies that week is a best unit for effective time management. Managers should prepare the list of tasks for the whole week. Then tasks should be classified on daily basis. These tasks should be prioritised on the basis of various mixes of importance and urgency. It is therefore suggested that HRD Managers should prioritise their tasks as under:

1. 'Musts' tasks
2. 'Shoulds' tasks
3. 'Ought/Might' tasks.

While planning the day and for making best use of time, managers should classify their activities in these categories. The 'musts' activities should be given top priority, followed by 'shoulds' activities. If time permits, 'oughts' may be undertaken.

Further, HRD Managers are responsible for many tasks. These tasks can be classified on the basis of their nature and importance and urgency as:

1. Important and Urgent
2. Important but not Urgent
3. Urgent but not Important
4. Neither Important nor Urgent

It has been felt that most of the time of HRD Managers is lost on activities which are urgent in nature. Thus many a managers find themselves entangled in performance of the activities which are important and urgent or urgent and not important and which are neither important nor urgent. A much less time is devoted on activities which are not urgent but important.

Urgency is a matter of time, hence managers are found busy in urgent matters, which have their own characteristics. But it has been experienced world over that majority of time of effective and successful managers are devoted to important and not to urgent activities. Importance requires systematic planning, which is found missing in most of the cases. If prevention is taken, crisis may be avoided. Ironically, managers are found managing the crisis most of the time. Such a situation needs change in working habits and style.

Managers have been found spending more time on directing, supervising (authority) and fire fighting (urgency) and paying little attention on planning, thinking, motivating and developing. This trend needs to be reversed. Managers should have mission and vision, priorities and importance.

Managing Personal Development

Every human being irrespective of his status and position has 24 hours at his command, not more, not less. Law of socialism completely prevails in case of time allotment. Instead of uniformity of availability of time, level of success is not equal. One's success depends upon effective use of one's time. Hence, time management is the soul of all managements. Controlling the time pre-supposes changes in habits. Habits are the inter-components of skills, knowledge and desires. Setting of goals is necessary for regulating time and life. Managers should therefore first set goals – organisational as well as personal, and pursue the right personal goals. Each of the goals should be allocated suitable time. Managers are required to utilize time compatible to life objectives. It has been observed that HRD Managers are much concerned about 'doing things right' and they do not emphasise on 'doing right things'.

It has been observed that HRD managers have set personal goals but they seem little unclear about them. Most of them are at the fag end of their career and they have reached to this level by virtue of length of service in the organisation and experience in the field. They are found satisfied with whatever they have achieved. Now, they are worried much about their children.

Most of the HRD Managers have no concern about managerial excellence and personal competence. However, they place themselves in right earnest in this regard. They feel fully equipped to meet the job challenges. They are aware of the objectives of their respective organisation. They however lack clarity of their roles. They find little place for enriching the jobs and developing the subordinates as every thing is supposedly pre-determined. Subordinates lack inquisitiveness and willingness to learn. They seem more interested in their promotion and increase in salary rather than the increase in capacity and capability. There is no mechanism except past experience and working behaviour of subordinates to assess the level of competence of subordinates.

Effective time management pre-supposes personal sense of time. It has been felt that HRD Managers have very little personal sense of time. Many of them are concerned about their time but have no respect for time of others, especially of their juniors and subordinates. Managers although feel the need of managing time and confess to manage time at office as well as home, in reality, no management of time is practised by majority of them.

Managers are found little conscious about self development but are much concerned about their elevation in hierarchy. They lack in setting of personal goals and planning the achievement. Their priorities are determined primarily on the basis of urgency. They have not identified their best time but feel fresh in the beginning of the day.

HRD Managers don't classify time as committed, free, leisure and personal. Most of them claim to be overburdened but largest portion of their committed time is found being eaten away by desk work and meetings. The unmanaged routine work and uncontrolled and unplanned meetings keep them busy and that is the reason of their expressing over burdened of work. It has been observed that some times managers are really busy whereas at many times they sit idle with no work. This imbalance is found because of lack of proper planning of tasks and time.

It has been found that about six hours per week or 24 hours per month are spent by HRD Managers on commuting to and from office only. The time spent on travel during office hours as a part of discharge of their duty is not included in this. The travel time is uselessly spent by most of the managers. Many do read newspapers, magazines etc. during travel time, while many relax. Managers should plan use of travel time as well.

Managers devote little amount of time to future planning and strategic planning which is the backbone of management. They claim to have every thing pre-determined either by the government or by the management board, hence feel no need to plan, but the managers should have set some goals and plan the days and weeks to achieve these goals. This requires systematic planning and its periodical review. This will become a reality only when managers set some personal mission and vision in life.

The committed time of HRD Managers is influenced by boss-imposed time, system-imposed time and self-imposed time. The demands of boss-imposed and system-imposed times bear penalties and managers cannot afford their delayed compliance. For maintaining a smooth balance and inter-relationship between these three times, the HRD Managers have to control the timing and content of what they do. Many managers prefer to wait until told, such tendency keeps lowest initiative. HRD Managers should therefore take resulting actions and routinely report. This is the highest initiative. HRD Managers should therefore act professionally. By adopting this style of functioning, HRD Managers can have full control over timing and its content. Unfortunately, HRD Managers are found behaving other way and confine only to carryout the directives from up and desist from taking initiatives.

HRD Managers are always flooded with piles of papers. In real sense public sector organisations run through papers only. It has been thus, observed that HRD managers spend lot of time on paper works – disposing of papers and responding papers. The whole exercise is totally unproductive yet part of functioning. It is therefore suggested that HRD Managers should reduce paper work. For the purpose they should delegate decision making so that all papers do not reach to them. They should handle a paper only once and should reply on original papers only. The informations can be obtained telephonically rather than creating paper works. Every attempt should be made to minimize paper work. Use of modern automation techniques should be optimized for less paper work and speedy action.

It has been observed that HRD managers spend a good part of their time either on holding meetings or attending meetings. These meetings are generally feedback meeting or monitoring meeting. At these meetings past is discussed, whereas past is history and cannot be changed. Meetings are however a necessary instrument for managing the things. HRD Managers should therefore make the meetings productive. For the purpose agenda for discussion be prepared and distributed amongst members in advance. Minutes should be prepared and followed up. Every attempt should be made to start meetings at scheduled time and finish at the determined time. Managers should not fascinate to hold meetings. Timing of holding meetings should be fitted some where in between 'must' tasks and 'should' tasks.

HRD Managers are found to have two levels of energy; one in the forenoon (between 9 to 11) and second in the late afternoon (between 4 to 6), the highest being in the forenoon. It is therefore suggested that important works be performed during this duration when the energy level is high. As regards energy level for the week, Friday and Wednesday have been found to have the highest level of energy, followed by Thursday and Tuesday. It is clear from the analysis that HRD Managers are applying only half of their energy level.

The top management should take note of it and create such an environment in which managers can put in more energy for increased productive use of time. Although managers are found busy all the time and they claim to put in about 6 out of 8 hours in active working, the actual energy of level used is about half. It needs to be optimized and one important measure may be effective use to time.

Managing Manager-Leader

HRD Managers are now not responsible only for performing the traditional personnel functions but also to leading a team. HRD Managers of today are manager-leader. Their responsibilities are motivating and developing the individual, achieving the tasks and building and maintaining the team. HRD Managers are thus leader, manager and professional, a unique combination of all the three. His dual personality as an employee and as a citizen adds another dimension. Thus the modern public manager has to work in multi-dimensional environment – internal as well as external.

Public sector in India in post-liberalised economy is facing a threat to survival. The managers have to adapt to the changing situation. The emerging challenges of privatisation and denationalization have resulted into intensive competitiveness. Deeply held beliefs of public sector are now challenged. The management of public sector managers and employees working in public sector enterprises are facing challenges of adaptation. In the changing environment, HRD Managers as manager-leader have their responsibilities diversified in areas related to organisation, team and own. He has the responsibility to his organisation to help achieve goals of organisation and realise vision. He is responsible for developing his subordinates in addition to ensure his own development.

While leading adaptive work, HRD Managers should have an overview of team working and should not be a part of the team exercise. He should first identify the adaptive challenges and then regulate the distress. Unfortunately, public sector enterprises as a whole have chosen the path of restraint rather than change. They are rigid in approach, incur losses, hence disinvestment is being practised. HRD Managers should maintain disciplined attention and always should give work back to people rather than keeping the ball in own court. Managers should protect voices from below. It is important that there is very little scope for taking initiative. Rigid rules prohibit initiatives. There is no mechanism to assess the potential of subordinates. The performance appraisal mechanism is neither objective nor development oriented. The most time of HRD Managers is lost in managing conflicts.

The public sector framework does not provide much scope for learning. The managers are also not conscious about learning and acquiring knowledge. They become part of the whole system and always clamour for advancement of career which has direct linkage with the length of service put in the organisation rather than merit and potential. Most of the managers are Reflector and Theorist rather than Pragmatist.

HRD Managers do believe, in principle, in team-building and team working, but there is no much scope in the rigid system of public sector enterprises. HRD Managers should therefore involve employees. Managers should practice delegation of powers and authority of decision making at the lowest level. They should invite the views of subordinates and honour them. Participative decision making is necessary at the operational level so that the employees who are responsible for execution are involved.

Unfortunately, lack of confidence and rigid rules constrain delegation. Employees of public sector enterprises can be involved only when the monetary incentives exist. The HRD managers are generally not empowered to grant monetary incentives. Non-monetary incentives fail to make any dent in the behaviour of employees. HRD Managers are found cautious while sharing the information with subordinates. Employees are seldom involved in identifying conflict areas. Minor conflicts are generally not taken seriously which over a period of time become major industrial problems.

It is therefore suggested that HRD Managers should empower their subordinates to take operational decisions. Informations should be shared with them. Their help in identifying conflict areas and suggesting redressal measures should be invited and paid due attention. HRD Managers are found favouring use of persuasion instead of authority in getting the works done. However, the objectives are not clarified, hence no specific mission. This adversely affects empowerment of subordinates.

HRD Managers agree to the principle of right man for right job, but in practice they are found miserably failed. The abundant availability of unemployed attracts the organisations to select highly qualified persons. The managers should appoint suitable persons but, there are no indicators to assess suitability. It requires drastic change in recruitment policy in public sector enterprises. Over-qualified as well as under-qualified persons are problem to the organisation. Hence only persons suitable to job requirements should be hired.

HRD Managers have to act as trainer and developer also. It is unfortunate that there is no comprehensive training policy in public sector enterprises. HRD Managers feel handicapped in this regard and some limited internal training facilities are made available in some enterprises. The arrangements are not adequate. There is a strong plea for training and development of employees.

It has been observed that HRD Managers behave like managers and not as a leader. The present situation demands a change in attitude and working style of managers. They should see a vision, set a mission, clarify the goals and roles, prioritise the tasks on the basis of importance and plan their achievement. They should concentrate on 'doing right things' in place of 'doing things rightly'. Manager-leader believes doing things right to achieve his goals. This all require a constant focus on use of time.

Managing Decisions

Some management experts define management as decision making. Many others feel in same nerves that life is decision making. It is true that every action in life bears some sort of decision making. It has been observed that a major part of time of HRD Managers goes in decision making. Every HRD Manager has to be a good decision maker. Decision making is a conscious effort to select alternative use of available resources. In view of limited resources decision making is an effort to discriminate rationally among available alternatives.

The job of HRD Manager is very important and critical as the optimisation of resources (fiscal and material) depends upon the human resource, the sole responsibility of HRD Manager. Hence, every action of HRD Manager requires decision making. HRD Manager must set objectives for his unit and must evaluate results and give guidance to his subordinates. HRD Manager facilitates the availability of human resource as and when required by other managers in the organisation. He thus enjoys a special status amongst his peers and in overall organisational set up. Hence he should act as a role model in the organisation.

The activities of HRD Managers can be classified in three groups: routine work, opportunities and problems. It has been observed that most of the HRD Managers spend lot of their time on routine works and problem- solving. A little time is left for opportunities. The time spent on routine works is non-productive or less productive, hence needs to be reduced. Problems can be minimized if time is planned for opportunities. HRD Managers should plan accordingly. Time on routine works can be reduced through delegation, organisation of office work, reducing paper work and planning the day. Problems can be tamed if employees are involved in identifying problem areas, the minor problems are taken care of initially, and views of employees are invited and listened attentively.

The effectiveness in decision making depends upon 'time' of decision. Time is a vital factor in decision making process. It is therefore necessary that HRD Managers develop and maintain strategic sense of time. They should maintain a list of activities. The list should act as a guide 'to do first things first'. They should group the activities on the basis of importance and urgency as: must do, should do and might do.

It is found that HRD Managers casually prioritise their works, but even that priority is disturbed due to urgent directives from the boss or due to some crisis. In absence of any planning by HRD Managers, urgency disrupts priority. If there is a planning for the day, lot of cushion may be available for urgent matters.

It is felt that HRD Managers are over-cautious while making decisions. They generally evade decisions in the name of studying the problems exhaustively. They don't want to take full responsibility and instead make every effort to shift responsibility. Contrarily, in many cases HRD Managers take snap decisions in haste. Both the situations are not healthy and some times become disastrous. They find little scope for initiative in decision making as every thing is pre-determined in public sector enterprises. Making a decision beyond the prescribed scope may boomerang as is felt by HRD Managers. HRD Managers seldom make major decisions for fear of going beyond their authority. Decisions are generally imposed rather than taken by consensus. The whole process consumes a lot of time of senior officials including HRD Managers.

As regards areas of decision making, HRD Managers have limited role to perform in enriching jobs, role development, creating working environment, granting incentives etc. They do have important role in procuring employees, developing employees, appraising their performance, problem solving, redressal of grievances etc. They should perform these activities judiciously and effectively. Even in area of their jurisdiction, managers have no free hand and hence more time is lost in communicating with peers and getting informations from different sources.

HRD Managers refrain from delegating generously. Extent of delegation is prescribed under rules and HRD Managers cannot cross the limit. Moreso, employees are not rated upto mark, hence delegation of powers is limited to supervisory level only. There is thus a need to be flexible and scope of delegation should be widened. If delegation is not facilitated, a lot of time is spent by HRD Managers in waiting communications regarding decisions taken at upper level of management. For the purpose, HRD Managers should develop the capacity and capability of their subordinates and then effect delegation.

Managing Own self

HRD Managers in many cases are at the fag end of their career. They are facing constraints of time, because demands are increasing and time is squeezing. They feel nearer to end of life and start feeling importance of time. Time management is virtually management of self. If HRD Managers plan their time, if they manage their life, they succeed in managing their time. In real sense, time is not managed but life is managed. Once life is managed, time is managed at its own.

Punctuality is a big step in the area of time management. Punctuality in all walks of life is a necessity. HRD Managers are in general punctual in reaching office as well as attending office works. But many of them are not so punctual in their personal life, in social life, and in their household responsibility. This adversely affects their time planning.

For effective management of time, HRD Managers are required to change their habits to a great extent. The problems being faced by HRD Managers generally fall into three areas: direct control, indirect control or no control. Direct control problems can be solved by change in behaviour. For the purpose HRD Managers should be pro-active, begin with the end in mind, and put first things first. Indirect control problems involve other people's behaviour. Managers can regulate such a situation by thinking win-win, seeking first to understand then to be understood and synergizing. For no control problems nothing can be done. They can be controlled by sharpening the saw i.e. by upgrading skills. Adopting these seven habits can make HRD Managers highly effective.

HRD Managers are first human being, then managers. Like other human beings, managers also have certain instincts, which influence their behaviour and life style. These dimensions are: physical, mental, emotional and spiritual. HRD Managers have to take care of all these dimensions of life. None of these four dimensions is less important. All are equally important for self development.

For managing themselves, HRD managers have to organise themselves. The key activities for self organisation are identifying different roles, selecting goals for each role, scheduling and daily adapting. The managers should first identify their different roles at office, at home, and in society. The roles may be as himself, as son, as father, as husband, as supervisor, as manager, as trainer, as motivator, as friend, as social animal etc. They should then set goals for each role. HRD Managers should then allocate time for each role keeping in view the four dimensions of life. Such a daily planning is necessary for over all development.

HRD Managers are found concentrating in professionalism. They have little knowledge of sales, market, finances and internal and external environments. Managers are found squeezing their knowledge in the name of specialization and professionalism. They should develop themselves as a unique combination of a manager, a leader and a professional. As a complete organisation man, they can make quick and proper decisions which help in effective management of their time.

HRD Managers are found not analysing how they use time. They seldom set priorities and develop time use strategy. They are not accustomed to prepare a time plan and implement it.

It is interesting to note that HRD Managers pay attention to all dimensions of life. They are found spending a lot of their time on shopping and traveling. Phone calls and office work at home are major time wasters even at home. They spend little time on reading, planning household chorus and on children.

The leisure time of HRD Managers is spend either by sleeping, relaxing, watching T.V. or gossiping with friends and relations. Their commuter time is often a waste. Many managers are found reading newspapers, magazines etc. during travel time. A few utilizes this time by making phone calls or just relaxing. Managers can use this time on disposing of paper works, preparing list of tasks to be performed, prioritising them, making phone calls, seeking informations telephonically etc.

HRD Managers are found spending meagre time on writing, visualizing, planning and meditation. They allocate some time for health related activities and relaxation as well. HRD Managers claim to spend all the time beyond office hours on attending family, but reality is far from it. Just remaining at home is not sufficient. Managers should allocate specific time for each role at home.

HRD Managers should budget their time and review it. Time must be allocated for all dimensions of life. A balanced human life requires proper attention on health, relaxation, meditation, exercise, yoga, entertainment, and sleep along with work. HRD Managers should be 'resultaholic' and not 'workaholic'. They should not only be busy in doing work, but should work for achieving some result.

Thus it can be safely said that time management is neither a problem solver nor remedy of problems. Everyone should take it up as a fun. They should thus persuade their peers and subordinates to manage their time. Slowly, whole organisation should adopt effective management of time. A single individual cannot bring a visible change. There is a need to adopt integrated time management. Time management must be made enjoyable and pleasant and not a matter of tension. The tool for planning the time be simple and easily understandable (different models are annexed with proposed model).

Time management should be started and taken up as a fun in life. An effective management of time may bring qualitative change in life and life style. It should be enjoyed like anything. Quality of life is raised by managing time. Life can be made meaningful and fruitful by time management. Time should not be planned, life should be planned. If life is suitably planned, time will follow. Time becomes slave to a managed life. An effective use of time makes a manager effective in life. It does not have to be a complicated daily chore. Manager should keep it as simple as possible.

The Time Management Work-Sheet

There is no universally acclaimed time schedule that can fit all spheres of activity and individual requirements. The type of schedule that you adopt should depend on your lifestyle, job, goals, priorities and other environmental, requirements.

The specialists on Time Management however have developed various models/worksheets for the purpose of using time effectively. The Time Management Worksheet of any type is an invaluable tool for helping any one in any situation to maintain a habit of objectives oriented working.

Model I

Albrecht (1978) suggests a Worksheet which is merely a list of things to do, with every item of significance included, and with every item earmarked to indicate its relative priority. This is of course merely one arrangement of the list of things to do. (Annexure I) A Time Management Worksheet of this type or of any other kind suitable to need can be developed on daily basis.

Model II

Covey (1992) suggests a weekly Worksheet. (Annexure II) A manager should first identify his different roles to be performed during the week. Every role should have some definite goal. He should prioritise the activities on the basis of week and for a particular day.

Model III

Pearson (1988) centres around result and opportunities. His model is very simple. (Annexure III) He feels that 20 per cent of the work produces 80 per cent of the benefits hence more emphasis on major opportunities to be pursued and key results to be achieved.

Annexure I
Time Management Work-Sheet

Things to do this Week	*Priority*			*Notes*
	High	*Medium*	*Low*	

Source: Adapted from Albrecht, 1978:169

Annexure II
The Weekly Worksheet

Roles	*Goals*	*Weekly Priorities*	*Sunday*	*Monday*	*Tuesday*	*Wednesday*	*Thursday*	*Friday*	*Saturday*
1.Individual Personal Dev.									
2.Husband									
3. Father									
4.Son									
5.Manager									
6.Supervisor									
7.Decision Maker									
8. Any other									

Source: Covey: 1992:166-7

Suggested Model

Based on these models developed by experts, a simple work sheet (Annexure IV) has been developed. To begin with we can plan our activities for a week. In case we fail to adhere we can plan on daily basis.

Annexure III

Key Results and Major Opportunities Assessment

The Key results to be achieved in order of importance:

Time spent on them (ranked 1 to 5)

1. ☐
2. ☐
3. ☐
4. ☐
5. ☐

☐

The major opportunities to be pursued in order of Importance

Time spent on them (ranked 1 to 5)

1. ☐
2. ☐
3. ☐
4. ☐
5. ☐

☐

Annexure-IV
Suggested Model for Time Management

	Hrs.	*Monday*	*Tuesday*	*Wednesday*	*Thursday*	*Friday*	*Saturday*	*Sunday*
Role 1	7. a.m.							
	8. a.m.							
Role 2	9. a.m.							
	10. a.m.							
Role 3	11. a.m.							
	12. noon							
Role 4	1. p.m.							
	2. p.m.							
Role 5	3. p.m.							
	4. p.m.							
Role 6	5. p.m.							
	6. p.m.							
Role 7	7. p.m.							
	8. p.m.							
	9. p.m.							

Bibliography

(i) Books

Abe, Joseph M., Dempsey, Patricia E. and Basset, David A., (1998), Business Ecology (Giving Your Organisation the Natural Age), Butterworth, Heinemann, Boston

Adair, John (1986), Effective Teambuilding, Rupa & Co., New Delhi

Adair, John and Allen, Melanie (2003), Time Management and Personal Development, Viva Books, New Delhi

Adcock, Robert L. (1970), The Management Process: A Preliminary Statement of its Functions and Principles and a Survey of their use, (unpublished Master's Thesis), School of Business, Florida State University

Adler, N.J. (1997), International Dimensions of Organisational Behavior, Southwestern College Publishing, Cincinnati, O.H.

Aggarwala, Dharma Vira (1977), Hand Book of Management Principles and Practices, All India Directories Publishers, Chandigarh

Aggarwala, Dharma Vira (1984), Management, Deep & Deep, New Delhi

Albrecht, Karl (1978), Successful Management by Objectives, Prentice Hall Press, New York

All India Management Association (ed.) (1999), Indian Business (Strategies for Competitiveness), Amexcel Publishers Pvt. Ltd., New Delhi

Anderson, Nels (1961), Work and Leisure, Free Press, New York

Argyris, C. (1964), Integrating the Individual and the Organisation, John Wiley, New York

Armystrong, M. (1977), A Hand Book of Personnel Management Practices, Kogan Page, London

Bacon, R.J. (1961), Management Training: Aims and Methods, English Universities Press, London

Barnard, Chester I. (1968), The Functions of the Executives, Harvard University Press, Cambridge, Massachusetts

Bass, B.M. (1985), Leadership and Performance Beyond Expectations, Free Press, New York

Beaumont, P.B. (1993), Human Resource Management: Key Concepts and Skills, Sage, Newbury Park, C.A.

Beckhard, R. (1969), Organization Development: It's Nature, Origins and Prospects, Addison Willey, Reading, Mass

Beckhard, R. (1969), Organizational Development: Strategies and Models, Addison-Wesley, Reading M.A.

Beer, M. (1980), Organisational Change and Development: A System's View, Good Year, Santa Monica, C.A.

Bell, Daniel (1973), The Coming of Post-Industrial Society: A Venture in Social Forecasting, Basic Books, New York

Bennett, A. (1990), The Death of the Organization Man, Simon & Schuster, New York

Bennis, W. and Nanus, B. (1985), Leaders, Harper & Row, New York

Berne, Erick (1963), The Structure and Dynamics of Organizations and Groups, Ballantine Books, New York

Bevans, G. (1913), How Working Men Spend Their Spare Time,Columbia University Press, New York

Blanchard, K. and Johnson, S. (1983), The One Minute Manager, Harper Collins, London

Bliss, Edwin (1977), Getting Things Alone: The ABCs of Time Management, Charles Scribner & Sons, New York

Bolton, Lyndon (1924), Time Measurement, Van Nostrand, Princeton, N.J.

Boyatzis, R.E. (1982), The Competent Manager, John Wiley, New York

Bower, Marvin (1966), The Will to Manage, McGraw Hill, New York

Brown, J.A.C. (1963), Techniques of Persuasion, Penguin Books Ltd., Harmondsworth, Middlesex

Brown, J.D. (1973), The Human Nature of Organizations, AMACOM, New York

Bruzelius, Nils (1979), The Value of Travel Time, Croom Helm, London

Burns, J. M. (1978), Leadership, Harper and Row, New York

Chakraborty, S.K. (1980), Management by Objectives: An Integral Approach, The Macmillan Co. of India Ltd., Delhi

Chandra, Mahesh (1976), Management in a Controlled Economy, Tata Mc Graw Hill Pub. Co., New Delhi

Chapin, Stuart F. (Jr.) (1974), Human Activity Patterns in the City: Things People Do in Time and Space, Wiley, New York

Child, J. and Partridge, B. (1982), Lost Managers, Cambridge University Press, New York

Conger, Jay A. and Kanungo, R.N. (1998), Charismatic Leadership in Organisations, Sage, London

Conger, Jay A. (1985), Charismatic Leadership in Business: An Exploration Study, Unpublished Doctoral Dissertation, School of Business Administration, Harvard University

Conger, J.A.and R.N. Kanungo (1988) (eds.), Charismatic Leadership: The Elusive Factor in Organisational Effectiveness, Jossey Bass, San Francisco

Conger, J.A. (1989), The Charismatic Leader: Behind the Mystique of Exceptional Leadership, Jossey-Bass, San Francisco

Converse, Philip (1968), Time Budgets, in David Sills (ed.), International Encyclopedia of the Social Sciences, Vol 16, Mac Millan Co. and The Free Press, New York

Cotton, J.L. (1993), Employee Involvement: Method for Improving Performance and Work Attitudes, Sage, Newbury Park, CA

Covey, Stephen R. (1992), The Seven Habits of Highly Effective People, Simon & Schuster, London

Cowling, A.G. and Mailer, C.J.B. (1981), Managing Human Resources, Edward Arnold Pub. Ltd., London

Cribbin, James J. (1972), Effective Managerial Leadership, American Management Association, Inc.

Craif, R.L. and Brittel, L.R. (1967), Training and Development Handbook, Mc Graw Hill, New York

Cushway, B. (1994), Human Resource Management, Kogan Page, London

Cummings, T.G. and Molloy, E.S. (1977), Improving Productivity and the Quality of Work Life, Praeger, New York

Dale, Ernest (1967), Organization, American Management Association, New York

Davenport, Thomas H. and Prusak, Laurence (1998), Working Knowledge, Harvard Business School Press, Boston

Davis, R.C. (1951), The Fundamentals of Top Management, Harper & Row, New York

Davis, K. (1977), Human Relations at Work, Mc Graw Hill Book Co.Inc., New York

Dayal, Ishwar (1976), Designing a Work Organisation, All India Management Association, New Delhi

De Grazia, Sebastian (1962), Of Time, Work and Leisure, Twentieth Century Fund, New York

Drucker, Peter F. (1954), The Practice of Management, Harper & Row, New York

Drucker, Peter F. (1964), Managing for Results, Heinemann, London

Drucker, Peter F. (1964-70), Drucker on Management, Management Publications Ltd., London

Drucker, Peter F. (1967), The Effective Executive, Heinemann, London

Drucker, Peter F. (1974), Management: Tasks, Responsibilities, Practices, Harper & Row, New York

Drucker, Peter F. (1999), Management Challenges for the 21st Century, Harper Collins, New York

Evert, R.M. and March, J.G. (1963), Behaviour Theory of the Firm, Mc Graw Hill, New York

Ernst and Young (1992), The Manager's Handbook, Warner, London

Filley, Alane and House, Robert J. (1969), Managerial Process and Organizational Behaviour, Scott, Foresman, Glenview III

Finningan, J. (1973), The Right People in the Right Jobs, Business Books Ltd., London

Fraisse, Paul (1957) 1963, The Psychology of Time, Harper, New York

Frankenhaeuser, Marinne (1959), Estimation of Time: An Experimental Study, Almqvist & Wiksell, Stockholm

Fryer, D.H., Feinberg, M.R. and Zalkind, S.S. (1956), Developing People in Industry, Harper & Bross, New York

Fulmer, Robert M. (1988), The New Management, Macmillan Pub. Co., New York

Gellerman, S.W. (1968), Management by Motivation, American Management Association, New York

Ghez, G. and Becker, G.S. (1975), Allocation of Time and Goods Over The Life Cycle, Columbia University Press, New York

Glueck, W.F. (1980), Management, The Dryden Press, Illinois

Gorlin, H. and Schein, L. (1984),Innovations in Managing Human Resources, Conference Board, New York

Goyal, R., Myers, Charles A. (eds.) (1967), Management of Personnel, P.C. Manak Tala & Sons, Bombay

Graham (Jr.) Cole Blease and Hays, Steven W. (1984), Managing the Public Organization, Washington D.C.

Gupta, S.P. (1979), Development of Managerial Skills in India, National Pub. House, New Delhi

Hagemann,Herald and O.F. Hamonda (1994) (eds.), The Legacy of Hicks: His Contribution To Economic Analysis, Rautledge, London and New York

Haimann, Theo, Scott, William G. and Connor, Patrick E. (1978), Managing the Modern Organization, Houghton Mifflin Co., Boston

Hamble, J.W. (1969), Improving Manpower Performance, Management Publications, London

Harbison, F. (1974), Human Resources: The Wealth of Nations, Oxford University Press, New York

Harris, Thomas A. (1969), I' M OK – You're OK, Sterling Publishers Pvt. Ltd., New Delhi

Harvey-Jones, J. (1993), Managing to Survive, Heinemann, London

Harvey Andrew S., Szalai, Alexander, et. al. (1984), Time Budget Research: An ISSC workbook in Comparative Analysis, Campus, Frankfurt and New York

Hesselbein,F., M. Goldsmith and R. Beckhard (1996) (eds.), The Leader of the Future: New Visions, Strategies and Practices for the new era, Jossey-Bass, San Francisco

Hickman, C.R. (1990), Mind of a Manager, Soul of a Leader, Wiley, New York

Hinrichs, J.R. (1978), Practical Management for Productivity, Van Nostrand Reinhold Co., New York

Hodge, Billy J., Johnson, Herbert J. (1970), Management and Organisational Behaviour, John Wiley, New York

Holley, William H. and Jennings, Kenneth M. (1983), Personnel Management (Functions & Issues), The Dryden Press, New York

Howard, A. (1995) (ed), The Changing Nature of Work, Jossey-Bass, San Francisco

Hunt, J.G. (1991), Leadership: A New Synthesis, Sage, New Bury Park, C.A.

Humble, John W. (1972), How to Manage by Objectives, AMACOM, New York

Humble, J.W. (1969), Improving Manpower Performance, Management Publications, London

Huseman, Richard C. and Goodman, John P. (1999), Leading with Knowledge (The Nature of Competition in the 21st Century), Sage, London

Kanungo, R.N. and Mendonca, M. (1996), Ethical Dimensions of Leadership, Sage, Thousand Oaks, CA

Kanungo R.N. and Mendonca, M. (1997), Fundamentals of Organisational Behaviour, Kendall/Hunt, Dubuque, IA

Kayastha, Sandeep (2000), Workload Reduction in Government, Excel Books, New Delhi

Kepner, Charles H. and Tregoe, Benjamin B. (1965), The Rational Manager, Mc Graw Hill, New York

Kepner, Charles H. and Tregoe, Benjamin B. (1981), The New Rational Manager, Princeton Research Press, N.J.

Kharb, Col. Karan (2003), Made to Lead, Wisdom Tree, New Delhi

Kilmann, R.H. (1984), Beyond the Quick Fix: Managing Five Tracks to Organisational Success, Jossey Bass, San Francisco

Kleemeir,Robert W. (ed.), Aging and Leisure: A Research Perspective into the Meaningful Use of Time, Oxford University Press, New York

Kobayashi, Shijeru (1971), Creative Management, American Management Association, New York

Kohn, Mervin (1977), Dynamic Managing, Cummings Pub. Co., California

Koontz, Harold and O'Donnell, Cuyril (1976), Principles of Management, Mc Graw Hill, New York

Koontz, H. (1971), Appraising Managers as Managers, Mc Graw Hill Co., New York

Kotter. J.P. (1982), The General Managers, Free Press, New York

Kotter, J.P. (1988), The Leadership Factor, Free Press, New York

Kotter, J.P. (1990), A Face for Change, Free Press, New York

Kriegel, Rand Brandt, D. (1996), Sacred Cows Make the Best, Burgers, Warner, New York

Lawler (III), Edward E. (1986), High Involvement Management, Jossey-Bass, San Francisco

Lawrence, Paul and Lorsch, Jay (1969), Organisation and Environment, Richard D. Irwin, Homewood III

Legge, K. (1995), Human Resource Management: Rhetoric and Realities, Macmillan, New York

Likert, Rensis (1961), New Patterns of Management, Mc Graw Hill, New York

Likert,Rensis (1967), The Human Organization: Its Management and Value, Mc Graw Hill Book Co., New York

Locke, E.A. and Latham, G.P. (1990), Goal Setting: A MotivationalTechnique that Works, Prentice Hall, Eaglewood Cliffs, N.Y.

Locke, E.A., Kirkpatrick, S., Wheeler, J.K., et. al. (1991), The Essence of Leadership, Lexington Books, New York

Mackenzie, Alec R. (1975), New Time Management Method for You and Your Staff, Dartnell, Chicago

Mackenzie, Alec R. (1975), The Time Trap, Mc Graw Hill, New York

Mackenzie, Alec R. (1975), How to Get More Done in Less Time, Mc Graw Hill, New York

Mali, Paul (1972), Managing by Objectives, Wiley, New York

Mathur, K.M. (1993), Towards Effective Management (Pathways to Excellence), Gyan Pub. House, New Delhi

Mayer, Jeffrey J. (1995), Time Management for Dummies, Pustak Mahal, New Delhi

Maynard, H.B. (ed) (1960), Top Management Hand Book, Mc Graw Hill Book Co., New York

Mc Conkey, Dale (1965), How to Manage by Results, American Management Association, New York

Mc Gregor, D. (1960), The Human Side of Enterprise, Mc Graw Hill, New York

Mc Gregor, Douglas (1967), The Professional Manager, Mc Graw Hill, New York

Meyerhoff, Hans (1955), Time in Literature, University of California Press, Berkeley

Milham, Willis L. (1923) 1995, Time and Time Keepers, Macmillan, New York

Mintzberg H. (1973), The Nature of Managerial Work, Harper & Row, New York

Moore, Leo B. (1968), Management Time, Industrial Management Review, Spring

Moore, Wilbert (1963), Man, Time and Society, Wiley, New York

Morrison, A.M. (1992), The New Leaders: Giddiness on Leadership Diversity in America, Jossey-Bass, San Francisco

Naisbitt, J. and Aburdene, P. (1985), Reinventing the Corporate Futura, Futura, Warner, New York

Nakanishi, Nasmichi (1963), A Report on the How-Do-People-Spend-Their-Time Survey: An Analysis of Livelihood Time of the Japanese, NHK Radio & TV Culture Research Institute, Tokyo

Nandler, D.A. (1997), Leadership and Change: The Case of Lucent Technologies, Delta Consulting Group, New York

Nanus,B. (1992), Visionary Leadership, Jossey-Bass San Francisco

Narayan, B. (1999), Project Management, APH Pub. Corporation, New Delhi

Needham, Joseph (1965), Time and Eastern Man, Royal Anthropological Institute of Great Britain and Ireland, London

Odiorne, George S. (1965), Management by Objectives, Pitman, New York

Odiorne, George S. (1987), The Human Side of Management, Lexington Books, Massachusetts

Olsson, David E. (1968), Management by Objectives, Pacific Books, Palo Alto

O'Reilly (III), Charles A. and Pfeiffer, Jeffrey (2000), Hidden Value (How Great Companies Achieve Extraordinary Results with Ordinary People), Harvard Business School Press, Boston

Patil, S.M. and Nigam, Raj K. (1981), Public Enterprise Management (Constraints and Autonomy), Documentation Centre for Corporate and Business Policy Research, New Delhi

Parker, Sharon and Wall, Toby (1998), Job and Work Design (Organising Work to Promote Well Being and Effectiveness), Sage, London, New Delhi

Parkinson, C. Northcole (1964), Parkinson's Law, Houghton & Mifflin Co.,New York

Pascale,R.T. (1989), Managing on the Edge, Simon & Schuster, New York

Pasmore,W.A. (1988),Designing Effective Organizations: The Socio-Technical Systems Perspective, John Wiley, New York

Pearson, Barrie (1988), Common Sense Time Management for Personal Success, Mercury Books, Livingstone

Perry, B. (1984), Enfield: A High Performance System, Educational Services Development and Publishing, Bedford Mass

Peters, Tom and Waterman, Robert (1982), In Search of Excellence, Harper & Row, New York

Peters, Tom and Austin, Jane (1985), A Passion for Excellence, Random House, New York

Peters, T. and Austin, N. (1983), A Passion for Excellence, Random House, New York

Porter, Lyman and Lawler, Edward (1968), Managerial Attitudes and Performances, Irwin, Homewood III

Porter, M. (1985), Competitive Advantage, Collier Macmillan, London

Quigley, J.V. (1993), Vision, Mc Graw Hill, New York

Rao, Panduranga (ed) (2001), WTO & Competitiveness (Challenges for Indian Business & Management Education), Excel Books, New Delhi

Robbins, A. (1991), Awaken the Giant Within, Simon & Schuster, New York

Robbins,H. and Finley, M. (1997), Why Change Doesn't Work, Orion, London

Robbins,Stephen P. (1979), Organizational Behavior (Concept and Controversies), Prentice Hall Inc., Eaglewood Cliffs, N.J.

Robert, Tom J. (1974), Developing Effective Managers, Institute of Personnel Management, London

Robinson, John P. (1977), How Americans Use Time: A Socio-Psychological Analysis of Everyday Behaviour, Praeger, New York and London

Robinson, John P. and Godbey, Geoffrey (1997), Time for Life: The Surprising Ways Americans Use Their Time, Pennsylvania State University Press, Park

Roddick, A. (1991), Body and Soul, Crown, New York

Rokeach, M. (1973), The Nature of Human Values, Free Press, New York

Sashkin, Marshall (982), A Manager's Guide to Participative Management, American Management Association, New York

Sayles, Leonard A. (1964), Managerial Behaviour: Administration in Complex Organisations, Mc Graw Hill Book Co., New York

Senge, Peter M. (1990), The Fifth Discipline: The Art and Practice of the Learning Organization, Doubleday, New York

Sethi, Narendra K. (1978), Managerial Dynamics, Sterling, New Delhi

Shackle, G.L.S. (1970), Decision, Order and Time in Human Affairs, Cambridge University Press, London

Shackle, G.L.S. (1958), Time in Economics, North Holland, Amsterdam

Singh, U.B. (1992), Human Resources Development, Rawat, New Delhi

Sorokin, Petirim A. and Berger, Clarence Q. (1939), Time Budgets of Human Behavior, Harvard University Press, Cambridge, Massachusetts

Srivastava, R.M. (1989), Financial Decision-Making, Sterling Pub. Pvt. Limited, New Delhi

Steiner, George (1982), What Every Executive Should Know About Strategic Planning, Free Press, New York

Steiner, George A. (1969), Top Management Planning, Macmillian, New York

Stewart, Thomas (1997), Intellectual Capital: The New Wealth of Organizations, Currency Doubleday, New York

Storey, J. (ed.) (1995), Human Resource Management: A Critical Text, Rautledge, New York

Storey, J. (1994), New Wave Manufacturing Strategies: Organisational and Human Resource Management Dimensions, Paul Chapman, London

Szalai, A., et.al.(1972) (ed.), The Use of Time, Mouton, The Hague, Netherland

Terry, George R. (1958), Principles of Management, Richard D. Irwin, Illinois

Thomas, Philip R. with K.R. Martin (1991), Getting Competitive: Middle Managers and the Cycle Time Ethic, Mc Graw Hill Inc., New York

Thomas, Philip R. (1989), Competitiveness through Total Cycle Time, Mc Graw Hill, New York

Treacy, Deelan Revised by Polly Bird (2002), Time Management in a Week, Hodder & Stoughton, London

Trichy, N. M. and Devanna, M.A. (1986), The Transformational Leader, Wiley, New York

Trichy, N. M. and Sherman, S. (1993), Control your Destiny, or Some one Else will, Currency Doubleday, New York

Tobata, Seiichi (ed) (1966), The Modernisation of Japan, Institute of Asian Economic Affairs, Tokyo

United Nations Educational Scientific and Cultural Organisation (1966),The Multinational Comparative Time Budget Research Project, European Coordination Centre for Research and Documentation in Social Sciences, Vienna

Urwick, Lyndell F. (1938), Scientific Principles and Organization, American Management Association, New York

Vroom, V.H. and Yetton, P.W. (1973), Leadership and Decision Making, University of Pittsburgh Press, Pittsburgh

Waters, Donald (1999), 101 Ways to Improve Business Performance, Kogan Page Ltd., London

West, M. A. (ed.) (1996), Handbook of Work Group Psychology, John Wiley, New York

Wheelen, Thomas L. and Hunger, J. David (2000), Strategic Management Business Policy, Prentice Hall, New Jersey

World executives Digest (editors) (1981), Management-Japanese Style, Makali, Manila

Yoshino, M. (1969), Japan's Managerial System: Tradition and Innovation, M.I.T. Press, London

Yukl, G. (1994), Leadership in Organization, Prentice Hall, Eaglewood Cliffs, N J

Zuzanek, Jiri (1980), Work and Leisure in the Soviet Union: A Time Budget Analysis, Praeger, New York

(ii) Journals and Papers

Alexander, L.D. (1985), Successfully Implementing Strategic Decisions, Long Range Planning, 18, 91-7

Bajaj, B.L. (1998), Time Management, Prashasnika, XXV(1), January-July

Bandura, A. (1977), Self-efficacy: Toward a Unifying Theory of Behavioral Change, Psychological Review, 84(2),191-215

Bandyopadhyay, A. R. (1995), Public Administration in the Twenty First Century: Preparing for a New Society, Management in Government, XXVI(1-4), April 1994-March 1995

Basu,Ranjit(1999), Boom Time,Hindustan Times(HT Careers), New Delhi,March 11

Becker, G.S. (1965), A Theory of the Allocation of Time, Economic Journal, September

Bensley, M. E. (1965), The Value of Time Spent on Travelling: Some New Evidence, Economica, 32, 174-185

Bensahel, Jane G. (1979), Getting the Best Out of Your Time, International Management, June

Bhargava, R.C. (1999), Watch Your Step, Hindustan Times (HT Careers) New Delhi, March 11

Bullock, N., Dickens, P., Shapcott, M. and Steadman, P. (1974), Time Budgets and Models of Urban Activity Patterns, Social Trends 5,45-63

Chaturvedi, Mukesh (2000), All About Effective Communications, Hindustan Times, New Delhi, July 6

Cohen, S.G. and Ledford, G.E. (Jr). (1994), The Effectiveness of Self-Managing Teams: A Quasi-Experiment, Human Relations, 47, 13-43

Conger, J.A. (1989), Leadership: The Art of Empowering Others, Academy of Management Executive, 3(1), 17-24

Conger, J.A. (1990), The Dark Side of Leadership, Organisational Dynamics,19 (2),44-55

Davis, R. (1962), Time Uncertainty and the Estimation of Time Intervals, Nature, 195, 311-2

De Serpa, A.C. (1971), A Theory of the Economics of Time, Economic Journal, December

Dmitriev, A. S. and Kochigina, A.M. (1955) 1959, The Importance of Time as a Stimulus of Conditioned Reflex Activity, Psychological Bulletin, 56, 106-32

Douglass, Merrill E. (1975), Creative Use of Time, The Personnel Administrator, October

Drucker, Peter F. (1961), How to be an Effective Executive, Nation's Business, April

Drucker, Peter F. (1999), Managing Oneself, Harvard Business Review, March-April, 65-74

Evans, A.W. (1972), On the Theory of the Valuation and Allocation of Time, Scottish Journal of Political Economy, February

Goleman, Daniel (2000), Leadership that Gets Results, Harvard Business Review, March-April, 78-90

Gross, Daniel R.(1984), Time Allocation: A Tool for the Study of Cultural Behavior, Annual Review of Anthropology, 13, 519-58

Gulenschwager, Gerald (1973), The Time Budget – Activity Systems Perspective in Urban Planning and Research, Journal of the American Institute of Planners, 39 (Nov), 378-87

Halan, Y.C. (1999), The Dynamic Manager, Hindustan Times (HT Careers), New Delhi, March 4

Hays, Steven W. and Tyer, Charlie B. (1980), Human Resources Management; The Missing Link, International Journal of Public Administration, 2

Heifetz, Ronald A. and Laurie, Donald L. (1997), The Work of Leadership, Harvard Business Review, January-February

Heirich, Max (1964), The Use of Time in the Study of Social Change, American Sociological Review, 29, 286-9

Hibbard, Janet G. and Landrum, Robert K. (1978), How to Fight Time and Win, Personnel Journal, May

House, R.J. (1971), A Path-goal Theory of Leader Effectiveness, Administrative Science Quarterly, 16, 321-339

Kanter: R.M. (1989), The New Managerial Work, Harvard Business Review, November-December, 85-92

Kastenbaum, Robert (1961), The Dimensions of Future Time Perspective: An Experimental Analysis, Journal of General Psychology, 65, 203-118

Leshan, Lawrence L. (1952), Time Orientation and Social Class, Journal of Abnormal and Social Psychology, 47, 589-92

Likert R. and Seashore, S.E. (1963), Making Cost Control Work, Harvard Business Review, 41(6), 96-108

Mackenzie, Alec R. and Kau, Dennis Le (1977), Take a Quick Hour....For Time to Think and Plan, American Society for Training Directors, June

Maini, Charu (2002), A Whole New Ball Game, Hindustan Time (HT Careers), New Delhi, May 9

Meier, Richard L. (1959), Human Time Allocation: A Basis for Social Accounts, Journal of the American Institute of Planners, 25, 27-33

Mills, Ted, (1975), Human Resources – Why the New Concern? Harvard Business Review, March-April, 124-134

Mintzberg, Henry(1996), Managing Government Governing Management,Harvard Business Review,May-June 75-83

Nolan, Joseph (1975), Protect Your Public Image with Performance, Harvard Business Review, March-April, 135-9

Odiorne, G.S. (1974), Management by Objectives: Antidote to Future Shock, Personnel, 53 (4)

Oncken (Jr.),William and Wass, Donald L. (1999), Management Time: Who's Got the Monkey?, Harvard Business Review, November-December

Porter, W. Thomas (Jr.), (1978), Time and Self Management, Journal of Accountancy, June

Rao, T.V. (1981), How Managers Can Sabotage Their Own Development,Indian Management, 20 (12)

Rao,T.V. (1982), HRD Practices in Indian Industry, Lok Udyog, 16(2)

Rao, T.V. (1983), Human Resources Management Japanese Style: An Experience, Vikalpa, 4(4)

Ratnam, V.G. (1971), Developing Managerial Effectiveness, Training Development, 7(4)

Rotenbury, Harry C. (1975), The Time Log, Management World, 4

Rotenbury, Harry C. (1978), Time Management and Communication, Management World, September

Rotenbury, Harry C. (1979), Time Management Scheduling, Management World, May

Saxena, Shailendra (2001), Integrated Time Management, Hindustan Times (HT Careers), New Delhi, May 18

Saxena, K.B.C. (1996), Re-engineering Public Administration in Developing Countries, Long Range Planning, 29 (5), October

Sengupta, Arjun (1999), Reforms & Development (Improve Efficiency of Public Sector), The Times of India, Lucknow, December 29

Shekhar, Chandra (2000), Testing Times for Public Sector, The Financial Express (Futurescope), New Delhi, January

Shekhar Chandra (2000), Testing Times for Public Sector, The Indian Express, New Delhi, January

Sidman, Murray (1956), Time Discrimination and Behavioural Interaction in a Free Operant Situation, Journal of Comparative and Physiological Psychology, 49, 469-73

Singh, N.K. (2000), Managerial Challenges of 2000: Opportunities and Threats, Prashasnika, XXVII(1), January-June

Stalk, George (Jr.) (1988), Time – The Next Source of Competitive Advantage, Harvard Business Review, July-August, 41-53

Szalai, Alexander (1966), Trends in Comparative Time-Budget Research, American Behavioural Scientist, 9(9), 3-8

Teal, Thomas (1996), The Human Side of Management, Harvard Business Review, November-December, 35-44

Index

P

Q

R

S